THE LOST ART OF

FORGIVING

THE LOST ART OF FORGIVING

Stories of Healing
from the Cancer
of Bitterness

Johann Christoph Arnold

The Plough Publishing House

© 1998 by The Plough Publishing House
of The Bruderhof Foundation

Farmington, PA 15437 USA
Robertsbridge, E. Sussex, TN32 5DR UK

First Printing 1997 - 5000
Second Printing 1998 - 10,000
Third Printing 1998 - 5000

Cover photographs
Background: AP / Wide World Photos
Inset and p.105: Hubert M. Stainton, Jr.

The photograph on p.25 is reprinted by permission
of Newsday, Inc. © 1997 Newsday, Inc.

A catalog record for this book
is available from the British Library.

ISBN 0-87486-950-1

Printed in USA

To MY WIFE, Verena,
without whose loving support
none of my books could have been written.

Contents

Acknowledgments

IT WOULD TAKE more than a page to list everyone who helped bring this book into print – there are dozens who worked on it, from those who typed the first draft to those who did the final layout and designed the cover. I thank each one, but especially Reuben Zimmerman, Emmy Maria Blough, Hanna Rimes, Ellen Keiderling, Hela Ehrlich, Chris Zimmerman, Emmy Barth, Dan Hallock, Emily Alexander, Clare Stober, Kim Comer, Jutta Manke, and Paul Hansford.

Most of all I would like to acknowledge those who allowed me to use their stories: Anne Coleman, Marietta Jaeger, Bill Chadwick, Steven McDonald, Chris Carrier, Elias Chacour, Bishara Awad, Naim Ateek, Joan Wilson, Joel Dorkam, John Plummer, Zohar Chamberlain, David Harvey, Michael Saward, and Michael Ross – not to mention many fellow members of my community, the Bruderhof. Your willingness to share has given this book a compelling personal dimension, and I am grateful to each of you.

Several of the names in this book were changed to protect contributors' identities. Where a first name appears without a surname, it is a pseudonym; all other names are real.

Foreword

WHAT DO YOU DO when your friend gives you a sawn-off shotgun?

For Roger, this was an easy question to answer. He used it. And he says that if he had the chance, he'd use it again. Roger's entire life has become consumed by an unquenchable desire to avenge his daughter's death.

Sarah had been out riding her bike when she was hit by a drunk driver. She died almost instantly. There was no doubt about who was to blame, and the driver – who didn't have a valid driving license because of a previous conviction for drunk driving – was sent to prison for manslaughter. But for Roger, this just wasn't enough. When the driver was released from prison, he borrowed a gun and shot him, fully intending to kill him.

The tables were now turned, and Roger found himself being charged with attempted murder. Astonishingly, given the fact that he had deliberately tried to take a man's life, he was acquitted. The jury found the driver – who had never once shown even the slightest remorse – so repulsive that they delivered a unanimous "not guilty" verdict. But in spite of having escaped a long jail sentence, Roger wasn't satisfied.

When I talked to him and his wife, Cathy, all they could think about was getting revenge on Sarah's killer. I asked Roger if squeezing the trigger and seeing the man collapse in agony, hit by a spray of lead shot, had made him feel any better. No, he said. Only killing him could make him feel better. I asked Cathy how she felt about it. "I could never be happy if Roger killed him," she said, "because that would mean that I hadn't killed him. I need to pull that trigger myself. I need to see him dead, and know I'm responsible."

Sitting with them in their house, I was overwhelmed by their heartbreaking sorrow. I cannot imagine the horror of their ordeal. And there is little doubt in my mind that justice was not served by the light punishment given to Sarah's killer, whose cold, self-centered callousness and total lack of remorse shocked me to the core. Yet I also couldn't help feeling even greater sorrow at the way their continued reaction to her death was compounding their misery. Having been through one hell, it seemed to me that their inability to forgive and let go was putting them through another. Every single day, they were being consumed by hatred and bitterness, as deadly as any cancer. Was this really what Sarah would have wanted for her parents – this living hell that was destroying their lives, but which had no impact on that of her killer?

Is there any way that people like Roger and Cathy can learn to forgive? Can they ever be released from the bitterness that tortures them? In *The Lost Art of Forgiving*, Johann Christoph Arnold tries to answer some of these questions. The book is full of stories of people who, against all odds, have found the strength to forgive those who wronged them, and in doing so have found peace: ordinary men and women like Gordon Wilson, whose daughter was killed by an IRA bomb at Enniskillen, and Phan Thi Kim Phuc, whose photograph – as a burned, naked nine-year-old caught up in the ravages of the Vietnam War – adorns the front cover of this book. It also contains stories of forgiveness a little closer to home: husbands and wives locked in a bitter quarrel, partners who've committed adultery, victims of childhood abuse.

Arnold retells all these stories with compassion and without judgment. They are moving and compelling, and no one who reads them will ever be quite the same again. They challenge us to explore a side of our nature that, if unchecked, threatens to devour us. But they also offer a way out of the tragic curse of bitterness and hatred. This book presents a vital message to those of us who find it hard to forgive others, or – as is so often the case – ourselves.

But don't take my word for it. Read on…

Steve Chalke
London, 1997

Prologue

Can Such a Man Be Forgiven?

THERE IS A HARD LAW…that when a deep injury is done to us, we never recover until we forgive.

Alan Paton

ONE MORNING in September 1995, as I sat drinking coffee and reading the local paper, I was horrified to see headlines reporting the abduction, in broad daylight, of a local seven-year-old girl. Over the next few days, I followed the story closely.

Within a week the girl was found in a wooded area only several hundred yards from the county jail, raped, sodomized, and beaten to death. Even worse, the man who confessed to the crime turned out to be an acquaintance of the child – and one she trusted.

The public's reaction was predictable: this man deserved to die. Under the state's new capital punishment statute, he was a prime candidate. Although the District Attorney had promised to reduce his sentence to a maximum of twenty years in exchange for information leading to the recovery of the girl's body, he went back on his word only days later, saying that he would have made a pact with the devil to find the child, and that he hoped to become the first DA in recent New York history to send a murderer to the death chamber. Residents interviewed in the local paper even suggested that the authorities release him so they could "take care of him."

While this rage was understandable, I wondered how it could possibly bring solace to the victim's grieving family. As a pastor, I felt fairly certain what my response should be: I arranged for representatives from my community to go to the funeral and sent flowers to the child's parents. I tried, unsuccessfully, to visit the family. But my heart still felt heavy. Somehow, I knew I had to visit the murderer – at this point still a faceless monster – to confront him personally with the horror of his actions, and to help him to the point where he was genuinely remorseful about what he had done.

I knew people would look askance at such a visit, if not misunderstand it entirely, but I was convinced it was my duty. So it was that a few months later I found myself sitting alone in the county jail, face to face with the uncuffed killer. The hours I spent in that cell shook me deeply and left many unresolved questions – questions, in fact, that eventually led me to write this book. Why should I, or anyone, forgive this man? What would it change? Could I forgive him if he didn't show remorse? And even if he did, would I have the right to forgive him, since he hadn't hurt me?

Less than three months after my visit, the murderer finally faced his victim's family. The county courthouse was packed and, entering it, one could feel a wave of hostility. The sentence – life imprisonment without parole – was followed by a statement from the judge: "I hope that the hell you now face in prison is only a foretaste of the hell you will face in eternity."

The defendant was then allowed a few words. In a loud, wavering voice, he told the girl's parents that he was "truly sorry" for the pain he had caused – and that he prayed daily for forgiveness. As a ripple of angry whispers spread through the audience, I asked myself the hardest question of all: can such a man ever be forgiven, anyway?

1 The Cancer of Bitterness and Resentment

WHOEVER OPTS for revenge should dig two graves.

Chinese proverb

FORGIVENESS is the way to peace and happiness. It is also a mystery, and unless we seek it, it will remain hidden from us. This book is not meant to be a practical guide to forgiveness – it is impossible to tell someone how to forgive – but I do hope it can help to illustrate why forgiveness is needed.

Forgiveness is possible. The stories in this book show how people have learned to forgive, even in the most difficult of circumstances. By retelling these stories, I hope to lead you to the door of forgiveness. Once there, only you can open it.

What does forgiveness really mean? C. S. Lewis said it goes beyond human fairness; it is pardoning those things that can't readily be pardoned at all.[1] It is more than excusing. When we excuse someone, we brush their mistake aside and do not punish them for it. When we forgive, we not only pardon a failing or a deliberate act of evil, but we also embrace the person responsible and seek to rehabilitate and restore them. Our forgiveness may not always be accepted, yet once we have reached out our hand, we cleanse ourselves of resentment. We may remain deeply wounded, but we will not use our hurt to inflict further pain on others.

When we re-visit a negative memory in the sense of chalking up another person's wrongs to us, it becomes a grudge. It doesn't matter if the cause of the grudge is real or imagined: the effect is the same. Once there, it will slowly eat away at us until it spills out and corrodes everything around us.

We all know bitter people. They have an amazing memory for the tiniest detail, and they wallow in self-pity and resentment. They catalog every offense against them and are always ready to show others how much they have been hurt. On the outside they may appear to be calm and composed, but inside they are bursting with pent-up hatred.

These people defend their indignation constantly: they feel that they have been hurt too deeply and too often, and that somehow this exempts them from the need to forgive. But it is just these people who need to forgive most of all. Their hearts are sometimes so full of rancor that they no longer have the capacity to love.

Almost twenty years ago, my father and I talked at great

length with just such a woman, trying to help her. Her husband lay dying, yet she was as hard and unfeeling as a rock. In the eyes of the world, she had lived a blameless life: she was neat and meticulous, hard-working, honest, capable, and dependable – yet she could not love. After months of struggle, the cause of her coldness became clear: she was unable to forgive. She couldn't point to a single large hurt, but she was bowed down by the collective weight of a thousand small grudges.

Bitterness is more than just a negative outlook on life. It is destructive, and also self-destructive. Willfully holding on to grudges against another person has a disastrous effect on the soul. It opens the door to evil and leaves us vulnerable to thoughts of spite, hatred and even murder. It destroys our souls, and it can destroy our bodies as well. We know that stress can cause an ulcer or a migraine, but we often fail to see the relationship between bitterness and insomnia, for example. Medical researchers have even shown a connection between unresolved anger and heart attacks; it seems that people who bottle up their resentment are far more susceptible than those who are able to defuse it by venting their emotions.

NOT LONG AGO I was asked to help a young woman called Brenda who had been sexually abused by her uncle, a minister. Although she was without question the innocent victim of a horribly depraved man, her misery seemed at least in part self-perpetuated. She would not and could not muster enough inner strength to forgive.

Silenced for years by fear of exposure and by her alco-holism – which her tormentor supported with daily gifts of vodka – Brenda cried out to me in despair. She had been offered intensive psychiatric counseling, and had every material comfort she could wish for. She had a good job and an extensive network of supportive friends, and every effort had been made to get her back on her feet. In spite of this, her emotions swung widely, from excited laughter to inconsolable weeping. She binged on food one day and fasted and purged the next. And she drank – bottle after bottle.

Brenda was perhaps one of the most difficult people I have ever tried to help. I was extremely hesitant to burden her with even one ounce of guilt, yet it seemed clear to me that only she could initiate the healing process. Until she could learn to start forgiving her abuser, she would remain his victim. But sadly, all our help was in vain. Angry and confused, she drove herself deeper and deeper into despair, and finally, after attempting to strangle herself, she had to be hospitalized.

The wounds left by sexual abuse take years to heal; of-ten, they leave permanent scars. Yet they need not result in life-long torment or in suicide. For every case like Brenda's, I know of others where the victims have found freedom and new life by forgiving their abuser and those who al-lowed the abuse to continue or failed to see what was going on in time to stop it. This does not mean forgetting or condoning – certainly it does not depend on a face-to-face meeting with their former abuser, which may be inadvisable. But it does mean making a conscious decision to stop hating, because hating can never help. Like a cancer, it can spread through a person until it completely destroys them.

SEVERAL MONTHS AGO I met Anne Coleman, a mother from Delaware who told me what had happened to her son Daniel, who could not forgive:

> When my daughter Frances was murdered in 1985, I was devastated. I received a phone call from my niece in Los Angeles, and she said, "Frances is dead; she's been shot."
>
> I can't remember screaming, but I did. I made plans to go out to California immediately, and on the plane I really thought I could kill someone: if I'd had a weapon and the murderer, I probably would have done just that.
>
> By the time I got off the plane I was getting concerned about how I was going to meet my son Daniel, who was flying in from Hawaii. Daniel was an army sergeant, and he had been trained to kill.
>
> When we got to the police station the next morning, the only thing they told us was that my daughter was dead, and that everything else was none of our business. Sadly, this remained the case throughout the days we stayed in Los Angeles. The violent crimes coordinator told me that if they hadn't arrested someone in four days, I shouldn't expect an arrest: "We just have too many homicides in this precinct – we spend only four days on homicides."

Daniel   Anne   Frances

This enraged my son Daniel. When he found out that the police department was really not interested in finding his sister's killer, he wanted to go buy an Uzi and mow people down.

They hadn't really prepared us for what we would see when we picked up her car from the pound. Frances had bled to death in her car. The bullets had passed through her aorta, her heart, both lungs. She had choked on her own blood. She died early on a Sunday morning, and we picked up the car late Tuesday afternoon. It stank. That smell never left Daniel's mind, and he wanted vengeance in the worst way. He really wanted someone to do something – some kind of justice for his sister.

Over the next two-and-a-half years I saw Daniel go downhill, and then I stood alongside his sister's grave to watch him being lowered into the ground. He had finally taken revenge – on himself. I saw what hatred does: it takes the ultimate toll on one's mind and body.

2 Overcoming Hatred with Love

HISTORY SAYS, *Don't hope*
On this side of the grave.
But then, once in a lifetime
The longed-for tidal wave
Of justice can rise up,
And hope and history rhyme.

So hope for a great sea-change
On the far side of revenge.
Believe that a further shore
Is reachable from here.
Believe in miracles
And cures and healing wells.

Seamus Heaney

GORDON WILSON held his daughter's hand as they lay trapped beneath a mountain of rubble. It was 1987, and he and Marie had been attending a peaceful memorial service in Enniskillen, Northern Ireland, when a terrorist bomb went off. By the end of the day, Marie and nine other civilians were dead, and sixty-three had been hospitalized for injuries.

Amazingly, Gordon refused to retaliate, saying that angry words could neither restore his daughter nor bring peace to his country. Only hours after the bombing, he told BBC reporters:

> I have lost my daughter, and we shall miss her. But I bear no ill will. I bear no grudge…That will not bring her back…Don't ask me, please, for a purpose…I don't have an answer. But I know there has to be a plan. If I didn't think that, I would commit suicide. It's part of a greater plan…and we shall meet again.[2]

Later, Gordon said that his words were not intended as a theological response to his daughter's murder. He had simply blurted them out from the depth of his heart. In the

days and months after the bombing, he struggled to live up to his words. It wasn't easy, but they were something to hang on to, something to keep him afloat in the dark hours.

He knew that the terrorists who took his daughter's life were anything but remorseful, and he maintained that they should be punished and

Gordon Wilson, 1994

imprisoned. Even so, he was misunderstood and ridiculed by many because he refused to seek revenge.

> Those who have to account for this deed will have to face a judgment of God, which is way beyond [my] forgiveness…It would be wrong for me to give any impression that gunmen and bombers should be allowed to walk the streets freely. But…whether or not they are judged here on earth by a court of law…I do my very best in human terms to show forgiveness…The last word rests with God.[3]

Gordon's forgiveness allowed him to come to terms with his daughter's sudden death, and its effect reached far beyond his own person. At least temporarily, his words broke the cycle of killing and revenge: the local Protestant paramilitary leadership felt so convicted by his courage that they did not retaliate.

EVEN IF WE RECOGNIZE the need to forgive, we are sometimes tempted to claim that we cannot. It is simply too hard, too difficult; something for saints, maybe, but not the rest of us. We think that we have been hurt one time too many, that our side of the story has been misrepresented, or that we have not been understood.

Many Americans have been moved by the story of Steven McDonald, yet few seem able to understand his act of forgiveness as anything other than a feat of supernatural will power. A New York City police officer, Steven was shot and paralyzed from the neck down in 1986 while questioning three youths in Central Park. He had been married less than a year, and his wife was two months pregnant.

Shavod Jones, Steven's assailant, came from a Harlem housing project; Steven lived in white, wealthy Nassau County. Their brief encounter might have ended with jail for one and life-long bitterness for the other. But even before Shavod had been released from jail, Steven started to correspond with him in an attempt to bring "peace and purpose" to the young man's life. He writes:

> Why he would shoot me had never been entirely out of my mind as I lay in Six South, looking at the ceiling. I was puzzled, but I found I couldn't hate him, only the circumstances that had brought him to Central Park that afternoon, a handgun tucked into his trousers.
>
> I was a badge to that kid, a uniform representing the government. I was the system that let landlords charge rent for squalid apartments in broken-down tenements; I was the city agency that fixed up poor neighborhoods and drove the residents out, through gentrification, regardless of whether they were law-abiding solid citizens, or pushers and criminals; I was the Irish cop who showed up at a domestic dispute and left without doing anything, because no law had been broken.
>
> To Shavod Jones, I was the scapegoat, the enemy. He didn't see me as a person, as a man with loved ones, as a husband and father-to-be. He'd bought into the cop myths of his community: the police are racist, they'll turn violent, so arm yourself against them. No, I couldn't blame Jones. Society – his family, the social agencies responsible for him, the people who'd made it

impossible for his parents to be together – had failed way before Shavod Jones met Steven McDonald in Central Park…

Some days, when I am not feeling very well, I can get angry. But I have realized that anger is a wasted emotion…I'm sometimes angry at the teenage boy who shot me. But more often I feel sorry for him. I only hope that he can turn his life to helping and not hurting people. I forgive him and hope that he can find peace and purpose in his life.[4]

Shavod didn't answer the letters at first, and when he finally did, the exchange fizzled out because Steven declined his request for help in getting parole. Then, in late 1995, only three days after his release from prison, Shavod was killed in a motorcycle accident on Madison Avenue.

When I visited Steven in his Long Island home several months ago, I was immediately struck by his gentle demeanor and sparkling eyes – and by the extent of his incapacitation. Life in a wheelchair is hard enough for an

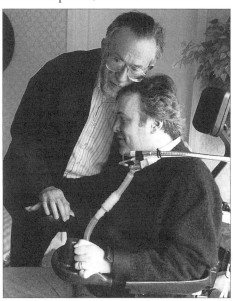

The author with Steven McDonald, 1997

elderly person to accept, but to be plucked out of an active life at the age of twenty-nine is devastating. Add to this a tracheostomy to breathe through, and a ten-year-old son you have never been able to hug, and you have Steven McDonald. But I sensed no anger, no bitterness.

Quietly but firmly, he poured out his heart, explaining how the shooting had forced him to re-evaluate his life as a whole:

> At first, forgiveness was a way of moving on, a way of putting the terrible accident behind me. But later I realized that I had been leading a selfish life, and needed forgiveness myself. It was that simple.

Steven has found purpose and meaning by teaching forgiveness. He speaks regularly in elementary schools, in high schools, and at graduation ceremonies. He sees this work as a God-given task.

Eleven years after the shooting, Steven's wife Patti is still faithfully at his side. They struggle daily with the reality of his disability and its effects on their marriage. Steven often has to fight back discouragement, and has even battled thoughts of suicide. But when I asked him if forgiveness itself was a struggle, he said no – it was a gift.

To forgive when one has been so severely injured cannot be easy. Yet even in the deepest agony we are faced with a choice: to love or to hate, to forgive or to condemn, to seek reconciliation or retribution. Steven might have succumbed to bitterness, but because he chose the path of peace and reconciliation, he is changing lives to this day.

One of his heroes is Martin Luther King, Jr. During our

visit he asked his nurse to hold up for him a collection of the civil rights leader's words, from which he read a favorite line: "Forgiveness is not an occasional act. It is a permanent attitude."[5]

CHRIS CARRIER forgave a man most of us would wish dead. As a ten-year-old in Miami, he was abducted and assaulted by a former employee of his father's and left to die in the Florida Everglades. He writes:

> Friday, December 20, 1974, was no ordinary day. It was the last day of school before the Christmas holidays, and we got out early.
>
> I stepped off the bus at 1:15 p.m. and began to walk home. An older-looking man who happened to be walking towards me on the sidewalk appeared to recognize me. Just two houses away from home, he introduced himself as a friend of my father. He told me he was hosting a party for my father and asked if I would help him with some decorations.
>
> I agreed and walked back up the street with him to the local youth center where he had parked his motor home. Once inside the vehicle, I put down my things and made myself comfortable.
>
> The Miami I knew quickly disappeared as he drove north. In an area removed from suburban traffic, he stopped on the side of the road. He claimed that he had missed a turn. He handed me a map, instructing me to look for a certain number, and went into the back of the motor home "to get something."

As I studied the map and waited, I felt a quick sting in the shoulder, and then another. I turned around to see him standing behind me with an ice pick in his hand. Then he pulled me out of my seat and onto the floor. Kneeling over me, he stabbed me in the chest several times. I pleaded with him to stop and promised him that if he would let me go, I wouldn't say anything.

I was immeasurably relieved when he stood up. He told me that he was going to drop me off somewhere, after which he would call my father and let him know where I was. He allowed me to sit in the back of the motor home as he drove. Yet I was painfully aware that this situation was beyond my control. When I asked him why he was doing this to me, he said that my father had "cost him a great deal of money."

After driving for another hour or so, he turned onto a dusty side road. He told me this was where my father would pick me up. We walked out together into the bushes and I sat down where he told me I should sit. The last thing I remembered was him walking away.

Six days later, on the evening of December 26, Chris was found by a local deer hunter. His head was bloody and his eyes were black. He had been shot through the head. Miraculously, there was no brain damage, but he didn't remember being shot.

In the months that followed, he struggled daily with the insecurity of knowing that his abductor was still at large. He also had to come to terms with the physical limitations caused by his wounds: he was now blind in one eye and could not take part in contact sports. And as any teenager would, he worried about his appearance.

Chris resented public mention of his survival, and remembers wondering how this "miracle" could have left him so miserable. Amazingly, at the age of thirteen, he underwent a change. He began to see his nightmare differently. He realized his injuries could have been much worse – in fact, he could have died. He also recognized that he could not stay angry forever. He decided to turn his back on animosity, revenge, and self-pity forever.

Chris Carrier, 1996

Then, on September 3, 1996, Chris received a phone call that changed his life once again. A detective from the Coral Gables police department called him at home to notify him that a man named David McAllister had confessed to being his abductor. David had worked as a physical aide for an elderly uncle in Chris's family. He had been fired on account of his drinking problems. Chris visited David the following day.

> When I visited him that afternoon, I felt an overwhelming compassion for the man. David McAllister was no longer an intimidating abductor. He was, instead, a frail seventy-seven-year-old who weighed little more than sixty pounds. Glaucoma had left him blind, and his body had been ruined by alcoholism and smoking. He had no family and no friends. He was a man who faced death with only his regrets to keep him company.

When I first spoke to David, he was rather callous. I suppose he thought I was another police officer. A friend who had accompanied me wisely asked him a few simple questions that led to him admitting that he had abducted me. He then asked, "Did you ever wish you could tell that young boy that you were sorry for what you did?" David answered emphatically, "I wish I could."

That was when I introduced myself to him. Unable to see, he clasped my hand and told me he was sorry for what he had done to me. In return, I offered him my forgiveness and friendship.

Chris says it wasn't hard for him to forgive, but the media still doesn't understand why or how he did it. They admired his ability to forgive, but could not understand what compelled him. They always went blank when the subject of forgiveness came up; it seemed they would rather focus on the drama of his abduction and the details of his torture. But Chris writes:

There is a very pragmatic reason for forgiving. When we are wronged, we can either respond by seeking revenge, or we can forgive. If we choose revenge, our lives will be consumed by anger. When vengeance is served, it leaves one empty. Anger is a hard urge to satisfy and can become habitual. But forgiveness allows us to move on.

There is also a more compelling reason to forgive. Forgiveness is a gift – it is mercy. It is a gift that I have received and also given away. In both cases, it has been completely satisfying.

In the days that followed this dramatic meeting, Chris began to visit David as often as he could, usually with his wife and two daughters. The two men spent hours talking, and the old man's hardness gradually melted away. Then, one evening three weeks later, just hours after Chris tucked his ailing friend into bed for the night, David died.

Gordon, Chris and Steven's stories show, perhaps better than any others in this book, the contradictions in the mystery we call "forgiveness." Most of us find it extremely difficult to let go even of relatively small grudges, yet these three men, who suffered beyond their worst nightmares, were able to forgive with almost unbelievable ease. Maybe this has less to do with them than with their belief in a higher power. In the end, all these men drew their strength to forgive not only from their own search for peace, but also from their faith in God.

3 Ending the Cycle of Hatred

IF ONLY THERE WERE evil people somewhere insidiously committing evil deeds, and it were necessary only to separate them from the rest of us and destroy them. But the line dividing good and evil cuts through the heart of every human being. And who is willing to destroy a piece of his own heart?

Aleksandr Solzhenitsyn

TAUGHT TO US as children, the familiar words of the Lord's Prayer give comfort to many of us, especially in times of difficulty or crisis: "forgive us as we forgive others." But how seriously do we actually take the message of these words: that we will find the strength to forgive when we recognize our own need for forgiveness? This recognition does not come to us easily. It always seems safer, somehow, to cling valiantly to our self-righteousness.

To explain the meaning of the Lord's Prayer, Jesus told the following story:

A rich man wanted to settle accounts with his servants. One of them, who owed him several thousand pounds, was brought in front of him, unable to pay. Because he was defaulting on the loan, the rich man ordered that the servant should be sold into slavery, together with his wife and children, to repay the debt. Although the rich man was within his legal rights to demand this, the servant begged him for patience. So the rich man took pity on him. He canceled the debt and let him go. But the experience left the servant badly shaken, worried about the state of his finances, and no sooner had he returned home than he went to a friend, who still owed him a small amount of money, and demanded repayment. His friend was also unable to pay, and begged the servant for mercy but he refused. Instead, he had his friend thrown into prison.

When the other servants saw what he had done, they were very upset and told the rich man everything. The rich man was furious, and called him in to answer for his actions: "You begged me to cancel your debt, so I did. Why didn't you show the same level of mercy to your friend as I showed to you?" In his anger, the rich man turned him over to the jailers to be tortured, until he could pay back all he owed.

The strongest motivation for forgiveness is always our own experience of having been forgiven, and our awareness of how badly we need forgiveness for the wrong we have done other people.

JARED, AN AFRICAN-AMERICAN college student from Boston, tells the story of his own battle to forgive:

> I was six years old when I awoke to the reality of racism: from the sheltered environment of my home, I was pushed out into the world – a local elementary school just down the road from our house. I went there for only a month before city law mandated that I be bussed across town to another school. My parents were not happy with this; they wanted me to go to a school where I was known and loved. They owned a farm out in the country, and so we moved there…
>
> My father, a veteran of the civil rights movement, taught us love and respect for everyone – white or black. I did not see along racial lines. All the same, I was the only black child in the school, and many of the other children had obviously been taught to hate. Children can be brutal about each other's differences. They may begin with an innocent question: why is your skin brown? But then they start to laugh and mock, because they know that brown skin is somehow different; somewhere along the way they have been taught that it is not "normal."
>
> I felt out of place. I was a fish out of water, and these kids didn't make it easy for me. I especially remember one incident. I introduced one of my white friends to another white kid on the bus one day, and from then on they always sat together but left me out.
>
> Then, when I was in the seventh grade in the city, there was a white guy in my class, Shawn, the only white in the whole school. We treated him as an out-

cast and taunted him with racial epithets and physically abused him. We took out our hatred of white people on him even though he hadn't done anything to harm any of us. We were angry. He symbolized everything that we knew about white people and their history: the humiliation of our people, the lynchings, the mobs, and the slave trade. We took out all our bitterness and anger on this guy.

I can see now that what we did to Shawn was wrong. We were racist, the very thing we despised whites for. Still today I ask for forgiveness for the harm I caused him. And I resolve to forgive the guys who didn't have the heart to love me when I was the only black kid in their midst.

H ELA EHRLICH, a Bruderhof member of Jewish descent, grew up in Nazi Germany. Her family managed to emigrate just before the outbreak of World War II and so escaped the death camps. But they suffered greatly, nevertheless. Her father died at the age of just forty-two, and she lost grandparents on both sides as well as all her childhood friends in the Holocaust.

She tells of her long struggle with bitterness and her continued unwillingness to forgive, which came to a head one day during a meeting of the whole community:

Hela Ehrlich, 1964

I sat down trembling, and as I did it dawned on me that if I looked into my own heart I could find seeds of hatred there, too. I realized that they are there in every human being. Arrogant thoughts, feelings of irritation toward others, coldness, anger, envy, even indifference – these are the roots of what happened in Nazi Germany. I recognized more clearly than ever before that I myself stood in desperate need of forgiveness, and finally I felt completely free.

JOSEF BEN-ELIEZER, another member of the Bruderhof, was born in 1929 in Frankfurt, Germany, to Jewish parents of East European descent. Like thousands of others, his parents had emigrated from Poland to escape persecution and poverty. There was little respite from either.

My first encounter with anti-Semitism came when I was only three years old. We were watching from our window at the *Ostendstrasse* when a formation of the Hitler Youth marched past, singing a song that even I understood: *Wenn Judenblut vom Messer spritzt* ("When Jewish blood runs from our knives"). I still remember the horror on my parents' faces.

Very soon, our family decided to leave the country, and at the end of 1933 we had moved back to Rozwadow, Poland, on the River San. Most of its inhabitants were Jews: artisans, tailors, carpenters, and merchants. There was a great deal of poverty, but under the circumstances we were considered middle-class. We lived in Rozwadow for the next six years.

In 1939 the war started, and within weeks the Ger-

mans entered our town. My
father and older brother hid in
the attic, and whenever someone
knocked at our door and asked
for them, we said they were not
at home.

Then came the dreaded public
announcement: all Jews had to
gather in the town square. We
were given only a few hours. We
took whatever we could carry –
just tied things in bundles to
carry on our backs. From the
square, the SS forced us to march

Josef Ben-Eliezer, 1946

toward the San, several miles from the village. Uniformed men rode alongside us on motorcycles. I will
never forget how one of them stopped and shouted at
us to hurry up; then he came up to my father and struck
him.

At the riverbank other uniformed men were waiting
for us. They searched us for valuables – money, jewelry,
and watches. (They did not find the sum of money my
parents had hidden in my little sister's clothing.) Then
they ordered us to cross the river, into a no-man's-land.
We were not instructed what to do, so we found lodging
in a village across the river.

A few days later we suddenly heard that this area was
also going to be occupied by the Germans. We panicked,
and with the little money we had hidden, my parents,
together with two or three other families, bought a horse
and wagon to carry the younger children and what little
we had managed to bring along on our backs.

We traveled east toward Russia, hoping to reach the border before dark, but found ourselves in a large forest when night fell. There we were attacked by armed men who demanded we hand over everything we had. It was a frightening moment, but there were a few men in our group who had the courage to resist them. In the end they left with a bicycle and a few other small items.

Josef's family spent the war years in Siberia. Miraculously, he managed to escape to Palestine in 1943. After the war he met Jews who had survived the concentration camps:

The first children freed from Bergen-Belsen and Buchenwald began to arrive in Palestine in 1945. I was horrified to hear what those young boys, some of them only twelve, thirteen, or fourteen, had gone through. They looked like old men. I was devastated…

I struggled with the British colonial occupation over the next three years. I was filled with hatred for the British, especially after they began to restrict the immigration of Holocaust survivors to Palestine. We Jews said that we would never again go like sheep to slaughter, at least not without putting up a good fight. We felt we lived in a world of wild beasts, and to survive, we would become like them.

When the British mandate in Palestine came to an end, there was more fighting for land between the Jews and the Arabs. I joined the army because I was convinced that I could no longer allow myself to be trampled on…

During a campaign in Ramla and Lod, my unit ordered the Palestinians to leave within hours. We didn't allow them to leave in peace but turned on them out of sheer hatred. We beat them and interrogated them brutally. Some were even murdered. We had not been ordered to do this but acted on our own initiative. Our lowest instincts had been released.

Suddenly, my childhood in wartime Poland flashed before my eyes. In my mind I relived my own experience as a ten-year-old, driven from my hometown. Here, too, were people – men, women, and children – fleeing with whatever they could carry. And there was fear in their eyes, a fear that I myself knew all too well. I was terribly distressed, but I was under orders, and I continued to search them for valuables. I knew that I was no longer a victim. I was now in power.

Josef soon left the army, but he still wasn't happy. He abandoned Judaism, and then religion as a whole, and tried to make sense of the world by rationalizing its evils. But that didn't seem to work. Eventually he came to the Bruderhof.

Here I experienced, for the first time, the reality of forgiveness. And I ask myself, how can I not forgive others when I myself need so much forgiveness again and again? Most of all, I am filled with the hope that one day people all over the world might be gripped by the same spirit that has saved me.

JARED, HELA, AND JOSEF had good reasons for not forgiving their enemies. Humanly speaking, they were innocent. The burdens they carried were the result of other people's prejudices and hatreds, not their own. In a sense, they had every right to feel the way they did.

I'm not trying for a moment to suggest that it is easy to forgive those who have massacred your family, friends and neighbors, but my overwhelming experience as a pastor and counselor is that those who are unable to forgive their persecutors remain their victims long after the physical pain or danger is over.

What's more, Jared, Hela, and Josef could feel themselves becoming just like the people under whom they and their families had suffered so much. They all found, as many others have found, that only by forgiving could they end the terrible cycle of hatred and free themselves from the horrors of their past.

4 Bless Those Who Persecute You

AT SOME THOUGHTS one stands perplexed – especially at the sight of men's sin – and wonders whether one should use force or humble love. Always decide to use humble love. If you resolve on that, once and for all, you may subdue the whole world. Loving humility is marvelously strong, the strongest of all things, and there is nothing else like it.

Fyodor Dostoevsky

IN THE SERMON on the Mount, Jesus said that we should love our enemies – in fact, he said, we should "bless" those who persecute us. This wasn't just rhetoric, as he showed so clearly and unmistakably with his words from the cross, "Father, forgive them, for they know not what they do." Stephen, the first Christian martyr, prayed much the same thing when his life came to a violent end: "Father, do not hold this against them."

Many people ridicule this, dismissing it as self-destructive foolishness. How can we embrace those who seek to harm or destroy us? When I showed an early manuscript of this book to my friend Mumia Abu-Jamal, a critically acclaimed African-American writer on Pennsylvania's death row, he reacted in just this way:

> It's easy for folks who live in a virtual paradise, who have enough to eat, farms, land, nice homes, businesses, etc., to preach about forgiveness. But, is it really fair to say that to people who live in hellholes – jobless, threatened by imminent death by starvation – people who are, as Frantz Fanon put it, "the wretched of the earth?" Are they to forgive the fat, well-fed millions who voted for their starvation? Who voted for war? Who voted for prisons? Who voted for their perpetual repression? Who wish, in their heart-of-hearts, that they were never born? Should they forgive them for the repression to come? For the genocide that is to come?

One person who thought they should forgive, however, was Martin Luther King, Jr. "Probably no admonition of Jesus has been more difficult to follow than the command to love your enemies," he wrote in his bestselling 1963 book, *Strength To Love.*

Some people have sincerely felt that its actual practice is not possible. It is easy, they say, to love those who love you, but how can one love those who openly and insidiously seek to defeat you...?

Far from being the pious injunction of a utopian dreamer, the command to love one's enemy is an absolute necessity for our survival. Love even for our enemies is the key to the solution of the problems of our world. Jesus is not an impractical idealist; he is the practical realist…

Returning hate for hate multiplies hate, adding deeper darkness to a night already devoid of stars. Darkness cannot drive out darkness; only light can do that. Hate cannot drive out hate; only love can do that. Hate multiplies hate, violence multiplies violence, and toughness multiplies toughness in a descending spiral of destruction…

Love is the only force capable of transforming an enemy into a friend. We never get rid of an enemy by meeting hate with hate; we get rid of an enemy by getting rid of enmity. By its very nature, hate destroys and tears down; by its very nature, love creates and builds up. Love transforms with redemptive power. [6]

King's commitment to love as a political weapon had grown out of his Christian faith, but there was also a streak of pragmatism in his thinking as well. He knew that he and his fellow African-Americans would have to live for decades to come in the same areas in which they were campaigning for recognition of their civil rights, denied them for almost two hundred years simply because of the color of their skin. If they let themselves become bitter about their treatment, it would spill over into vio-

lence, and that would simply lead to more bitterness and
resentment in the future. Rather than breaking down the
walls of racial hatred, it would build them up higher. Only
forgiving their oppressors could deliver African-Americans –
and white Americans – from the "descending spiral of destruction." Only forgiveness could point the way forward
to a brighter future.

> We must develop and maintain the capacity to forgive.
> Whoever is devoid of the power to forgive is devoid of
> the power to love. It is impossible even to begin the act
> of loving one's enemies without the prior acceptance of
> the necessity, over and over again, of forgiving those
> who inflict evil and injury upon us. It is also necessary
> to realize that the forgiving act must always be initiated
> by the person who has been wronged, the victim of
> some great hurt, the recipient of some tortuous injustice,
> the absorber of some terrible act of oppression. The
> wrongdoer may request forgiveness. They may come to
> themselves, and, like the prodigal son, move up some
> dusty road, their heart palpitating with the desire for
> forgiveness. But only the injured neighbor, the loving
> father back home, can really pour out the warm waters
> of forgiveness.
>
> Forgiveness does not mean ignoring what has been
> done or putting a false label on an evil act. It means,
> rather, that the evil act no longer remains as a barrier to
> the relationship. Forgiveness is a catalyst creating the
> atmosphere necessary for a fresh start and a new begin-
> ning…
>
> To our most bitter opponents we say: "We shall
> match your capacity to inflict suffering by our capacity

to endure suffering. We shall meet your physical force with soul force. Do to us what you will, and we shall continue to love you. We cannot in all good conscience obey your unjust laws, because non-cooperation with evil is as much a moral obligation as is cooperation with good. Throw us in jail, and we shall still love you. Send your hooded perpetrators of violence into our community at the midnight hour and beat us and leave us half dead, and we shall still love you. But be ye assured that we will wear you down by our capacity to suffer. One day we shall win our freedom, but not only for ourselves. We shall so appeal to your heart and conscience that we shall win you in the process, and our victory will be a double victory."[7]

In THE SPRING of 1965 I marched with Martin Luther King in Marion, Alabama, experiencing firsthand his deep love and humility in the face of terrible injustice.

I had been visiting old friends at the Tuskegee Institute when we heard about the death of Jimmie Lee Jackson, a young man who had been shot eight days earlier when a rally at a church in Marion was broken up by police. State troopers from all over central Alabama had converged on the town and beaten the protesters with clubs as they poured out onto the streets.

Bystanders later described a scene of utter chaos in which white onlookers smashed cameras and shot out street lights, while police officers brutally attacked men and women, some of whom continued to kneel and pray on the steps of their church. Jimmie's crime was to tackle a state trooper who was mercilessly beating his mother. His punishment was to be shot in the stomach and clubbed on the head until almost dead. Denied admission at the local hospital, he was taken to Selma, where he was able to tell his story to reporters. He died several days later.

At the news of Jimmie's death, we drove to Selma immediately. The viewing, at Brown Chapel, was open-casket, and although the mortician had done his best to cover his injuries, the wounds on Jimmie's head could not be hidden: three murderous blows, each an inch wide and three inches long, ran above his ear, at the base of his skull, and on the top of his head.

Deeply shaken, we attended the memorial service there, the first of two. The room was packed with about three thousand people (many more stood outside), and we sat on a window sill at the back. We never heard one note of anger or revenge in the service. Instead, a spirit of courage emanated from the congregation, especially as they sang the old slave song, "Ain't gonna let nobody turn me 'round."

Later, at Zion Methodist Church in Marion, the atmosphere was decidedly more subdued. Lining the veranda of the County Court House across the street stood a long row of state troopers, hands on their night sticks, looking straight at us. These were the same men who had attacked Marion's blacks only days before. The crowd of whites gathered at nearby City Hall was no less intimidating. Armed with binoculars and cameras, they scanned and photographed us so thoroughly that we felt every one of us had been marked.

At the cemetery, King spoke about forgiveness and love. He pleaded with his people to pray for the police, to forgive the murderer, and to forgive those who were persecuting them. Then we held hands and sang, "We shall overcome." It was an unforgettable moment. If there was ever cause for hatred or vengeance, it was here. But none was to be felt, not even from Jimmie's parents.

Going to Selma was not without danger. Only four days after the funeral, marchers en route to Montgomery were met with tear gas and mounted police who rode them down and beat them mercilessly. Two days after that, a white Boston clergyman, James Reeb, was savagely beaten in downtown Selma, dying from his injuries only two days later. Within the next three weeks, Viola Liuzzo, a white woman from Detroit, was shot and killed as she drove a black man home from a march. (We had done virtually the same thing only a week earlier, when we gave a lift to three women who needed a ride to Marion.)

Years later, I was deeply moved when I read about a remarkable act of forgiveness by the children of Selma in those same days of February and March 1965. Local students had organized a peaceful after-school march when the town's notorious Sheriff Clark arrived. He and his deputies began to push and prod the children, and soon they were running. Initially the boys and girls thought Clark's men were marching them to the county jail, but it soon became clear that they were headed for a prison camp almost five miles out of town. The men didn't relent until the children were retching and vomiting. Later they claimed they only wanted to wear out Selma's "marching fever" for good.

A few days after this incident, Sheriff Clark was hospitalized with chest pains. Unbelievably, Selma's school children organized a second march outside the Court House, this time chanting prayers and carrying get-well signs.

ROBERT COLES, the eminent American child psychiatrist, observed the same remarkable attitude of forgiveness among children when he was working in a New Orleans hospital in 1960. White parents, openly opposed to the Federal Court decision compulsorily ending segregation in the city's schools, not only withdrew their children from any school that admitted a black student, but picketed these schools as well.

One child, six-year-old Ruby Bridges, was the sole African American student at her school, which meant that for a while she was also the only student there. For weeks she had to be escorted to school by federal marshals. One day, her teacher saw her mouthing words as she passed the lines of angry white parents hurling abuse. When the teacher reported this to Coles, he was curious: what had she said?

When he asked her, Ruby said that she had been praying for the white parents. Coles was surprised. Why was she praying for them? "Because they need praying for," she answered. She had heard in church about Jesus' dying words, "Father, forgive them, for they know not what they do," and had taken them to heart. Coles saw in Ruby Bridges, and in those like her, the seeds of America's re-birth.[8]

THROUGH JAMES CHRISTENSEN, an acquaintance who is the prior of a Trappist monastery in Rome, I recently learned of a remarkable story of forgiveness before the fact. In May 1996, the G.I.A., a radical Islamic group in Algeria, kidnapped seven of James's fellow Trappists in the Atlas Mountains and threatened to hold them hostage until France released several of their own imprisoned compatri-ots. When the French government refused, the G.I.A. slit the monks' throats.

All France was horrified, and every Catholic church in France – 40,000 of them – rang its bells at the same time in the monks' memory. What struck me most deeply about the tragedy, however, was something that had quietly fore-shadowed it two years before. The prior of the Algerian monastery, Christian de Chergé, had had a strange premo-nition that he would soon die a violent death, and wrote a letter forgiving his future assassins. He sealed the letter and left it with his mother in France. Discovered only after his murder, it read in part:

> If it should happen one day – and it could be today – that I become a victim of the terrorism that now seems to encompass all the foreigners living in Algeria, I would like my community, my church, my family, to remember

that my life was given to God and to Algeria; and that they accept that the sole Master of all life was not a stranger to this brutal departure.

I would like, when the time comes, to have a space of clearness that would allow me to beg forgiveness of God and of my fellow human beings, and at the same time to forgive with all my heart the one who will strike me down.

I could not desire such a death; it seems to me important to state this – How could I rejoice if the Algerian people I love were indiscriminately accused of my murder?

For this life lost, I give thanks to God. In this thank you, which is said for everything in my life from now on, I certainly include...you, also, my last-minute friend who will not have known what you are doing... I commend you to the God in whose face I see yours. And may we find each other, happy "good thieves" in Paradise, if it please God, the Father of us both.

Clearly, this prior and his brothers were not only courageous men who accepted their deaths. There have been many of those. These men were filled with a spirit of rare humility and forgiving love that can only be described as Christ-like.

FEW PLACES ON THIS EARTH need reconciliation as much as Israel. I first traveled to this war-torn land in 1988, where I met Elias Chacour, a Melkite priest and Palestinian activist who for many years has worked tirelessly for peace. Our friendship lasts to this day, and Elias has visited our Bruderhof communities twice.

Elias might justifiably be expected to harbor bitterness. A "man without a country" ever since his home village was destroyed in 1947, he has been imprisoned more than once and has endured years of harassment and abuse at the hands of the Israeli government. Yet Elias is one of

Elias Chacour, 1990

the warmest, humblest, and most compassionate people I know. As a displaced Palestinian, he is nevertheless committed to the idea that, "The Jews deserve a homeland, not because they are Jews, but because they are human." On a recent visit to our British community, he reminded us:

> If my heart is full of forgiveness to the Jews, to the Zionists, to the soldiers who broke the bones of my brother and imprisoned my father – then I can go to that Jew and tell him the truth to his face, and he will feel that I love him, even if I dislike his injustice... I would rather call him to conversion than change roles and oppress him – God forbid!

NAIM ATEEK, a well-known Palestinian priest at St. George's Cathedral in Jerusalem, shares a similar outlook.

The author with Naim Ateek in Jerusalem, 1997

He learned forgiveness from his father, who lost everything to the Israeli army in 1948.

"When people hate, its power engulfs them and they are totally consumed by it…Keep struggling against hatred and resentment. At times you will have the upper hand, at times you will feel beaten down. Although it is extremely difficult, never let hatred completely overtake you…

Never stop trying to live the commandment of love and forgiveness.

Do not dilute the strength of Jesus's message: do not shun it, do not dismiss it as unreal and impractical. Do not cut it to your size, trying to make it more applicable to real life in the world. Do not change it so that it will suit you. Keep it as it is, aspire to it, desire it, and work with God for its achievement.[9]

L̲IKE SO MANY on both sides of the Arab-Israeli conflict, Bishara Awad, another Palestinian acquaintance of mine, has been wounded by his share of injustices. He recently told me about his life-long struggle to forgive:

In 1948, during the terrible war between the Arabs and the Jewish settlers, thousands of Palestinians died and many more became homeless. Our own family was not spared. My father was shot dead by a stray bullet, and there was no decent burial place. No one could leave the area for fear of getting shot at by either side; there was not a priest nor a minister to say a prayer. So Mother read to us from the Bible, and the men who were present buried my father in the courtyard. There was no way they could have taken him to the regular cemetery in the city.

Mother thus became a widow at the age of twenty-nine, and she was left with seven children. I was only nine years old. For weeks we were caught up in the crossfire and were unable to leave our basement room. Then one night, the Jordanian army forced us to run to the Old City. That was the last time we ever saw our home and our furniture. We ran away with nothing but the clothes on our backs, some of us only in pajamas…

In the Old City we were refugees. We were put in a kerosene storage room that had no furniture. A Muslim family gave us some blankets and some food. Life was very hard; I still remember nights when we went to sleep without any food.

Mother had been trained as a nurse, and she got a job at a hospital for $25 a month. She worked at night and continued

Bishara Awad, 1990

her studies during the day, and we children were put in orphanages. My sisters were accepted in a Muslim school, and we boys were placed in a home run by a British lady. To me, this was a real blow. First I had lost my father, and now I was away from my mother and my family.

We were allowed to visit home once a month, but otherwise we stayed at the boys' home for the next twelve years. Here, with my two brothers and eighty other boys, my suffering continued. We never had enough to eat. The food was terrible and the treatment harsh.

As an adult, Bishara went to school in the United States and became an American citizen. Later he returned to Israel and took a job teaching in a Christian school. Looking back, he says:

That first year I was very frustrated. I did not accomplish much and I felt defeated…There was mounting hatred against the Jewish oppressors: all of my students were Palestinians, and all had suffered in the same way I had…and I wasn't able to help my students because this same hatred was in me. I had harbored it since childhood without even realizing it.

That night I prayed to God in tears. I asked forgiveness for hating the Jews and for allowing hatred to control my life…He took away my frustration, hatred, and hopelessness and replaced it with love.

IN A SOCIETY that emphasizes self-preservation and individualism, the act of forgiveness is avoided, if not despised. It is even seen as a weakness; we are taught to assert our rights and protect them, not yield them.

But Raja Shehadeh, a Palestinian human rights lawyer, argues that Jesus turned this logic on its head when he called for people to forgive their enemies.

> The act of forgiveness carries a lot of power. It is an assertion of one's dignity to have the means and ability to forgive…It may be difficult to understand, but idealistically speaking, I think that if there is to be peace here, there has to be forgiveness…We have to forgive [the Israelis] for what they did to us.[10]

Far from leaving us weak and vulnerable, forgiving empowers our lives and our work. It brings true closure to the most difficult situations, for it allows us to lay aside the riddles of retribution and human justice and to experience true peace of heart. More than that, it sets into motion a positive chain reaction that brings the fruits of our forgiveness to others.

5 Forgiveness and Justice

TRUTH without love kills, but love without truth lies.

Eberhard Arnold

JOEL DORKAM, a good friend from Kibbutz Tsuba in Israel, experienced hardships similar in many ways to those of Hela and Josef, in Chapter Three, but offers a somewhat different perspective. He acknowledges the need for mutual forgiveness and mutual trust in the modern-day Israeli-Palestinian conflict, and as a Jew has taken risks to establish lasting friendships with ordinary Germans. But he is filled with anguish at the thought of forgiving the Nazis who ruined his childhood and massacred his fellow Jews. His story raises an age-old question posed by generations of suffering men and women over the course of human history: are there no limits to forgiveness?

I was born in Kassel, Germany, in 1929, the fateful year of the financial and economic crash that had such a decisive impact on world affairs and was instrumental in bringing the Nazis to power in Germany…My father was a journalist; mother an educator. Our family was well off, and life was happy until the clouds of Fascism began to accumulate.

Joel Dorkam

Like many Jews throughout the country, father did not take the Nazis too seriously at first. How could the solid, cultured Germans fall for that nonsense? But when Hitler became chancellor, well-wishing friends advised my parents to leave Germany.

So my father took leave of his beloved homeland, where he was born and raised, and for whom he had fought in the First World War. Mother and I followed shortly, and we were reunited at Strasbourg. We took with us only a few of our possessions. It was the end of our normal, accustomed way of life; we had become homeless, wandering Jews, without a nationality and without rights.

For me, a curious three-year-old, it was an exciting time. I quickly learned new customs, a new language, and I made new friends. But a year later we had to move again; as German refugees, we were considered a security risk in border areas. We went to a village in the

Vosges – another change. My parents had to learn new trades and a new language, to adapt to a very different culture, to do without most of the comforts of their previous lifestyle – and before that, to make a living under difficult circumstances…

A year later, the factory that employed my mother burned down, which necessitated another move, this time to Marseille. Again my parents tried to eke out a living, and they built up a rather precarious existence. We frequently changed apartments, which meant I frequently had to change schools and friends. I never had the chance to form lasting relationships…

Then the Second World War broke out, and everything went to pieces. I was a stranger again, and an alien one on top of that…France was invaded and then occupied by the German army, and soon the Gestapo were making arrests…Our apartment and my parents' business were confiscated but, with the help of French friends, we went into hiding.

Finally my parents decided that our only hope of survival lay in escaping over the border to Spain. Father was just recovering from an arthritis attack and had to walk across the Pyrenees leaning on two sticks, part of the time carried on the back of our guide…

After walking for three days through snow-covered mountains, with father repeatedly begging to be left behind, the Spanish *Guardia Civil* (border police) caught up with us. Luckily they let us through – as they did most of the nearly 10,000 Jews who illegally crossed into Spain. Had we been shipped back to France, it would have meant sure death…

As it was, we were torn apart at the Gerona police station. Father was sent to a camp in Miranda-del-Ebro, and mother to the local prison. I was left behind on my own. I spent the most miserable night of my life alone in a freezing cell, thinking I had lost my parents forever. The next day I landed in Gerona's orphanage, which did little to improve my spirits. There I turned thirteen (the age young Jewish males are solemnly received into the congregation of the faithful) – and missed my *bar-mitzvah*.

A warm-hearted priest took me under his patronage and comforted me in my hardest hours. He also smuggled some money I had secretly carried with me from France into mother's cell, where she lay gravely ill with dysentery and was unable to buy adequately nourishing food. That money probably saved her life.

After a few months I was sent to join my mother, and together we were transferred to a women's prison in Madrid. I was probably the only male in that place, and mother had to keep watch on me. We had a separate cell, while most of the other prisoners were kept in big dormitories with twenty to thirty beds. During the day we joined the women in these larger rooms, and walking back to our private cell in the evenings we passed the death cells where women awaited execution. At night we could hear the shots.

Some time later the whole family was reunited in Madrid. Our living expenses were covered by the Jewish Joint Welfare Committee, but there came a time when we had to make a choice as to our next place of migration, and we decided in favor of Palestine.

It was 1944, towards the end of the war, and conditions in the new country were hard. We shared a small flat with my aunt's family, and I enrolled in a trade school at Kibbutz Yagur and became an auto mechanic. The school had been built for Jewish-German children rescued from Europe, but by the time I arrived, there were no children left to rescue. So most of the students were *sabras*, local kids, and I – with my own background of an assimilated German-Judaism and only scarce knowledge of Jewish customs and traditions – was once again different, strange…

I slowly began to feel at home in the new country and on the kibbutz. I made friends and took part in various activities, like harvesting grapes and corn during the summer vacations. Yet many of my personal, professional, and social ambitions could no longer be realized; there had been too many gaps in my schooling. It was the same for my parents. My mother gradually taught herself Hebrew and found work at a nearby agricultural school, but my father never mastered the new language.

Once the war ended, life became more or less normal again. I finished school and became a member of the underground *Haganah*, fought in the War of Liberation, and then joined Tsuba (a kibbutz near Jerusalem) with my red-haired wife-to-be, Sarah, an Israeli-born *sabra*. I made a solemn vow not to wander anymore: this would be my home for the rest of my life, and here I would live and work and raise my children as part of the collective, trying to help immigrants who had gone through similar hardships.

Looking back on my childhood, I realize that it afforded me many useful experiences, and perhaps some wisdom. I learned (the hard way) how much people depend on one another, especially in times of hardship. I discovered the importance of a helpful deed and an encouraging word. I also came to realize that there are good and bad people everywhere, and that most of us actually are a combination of both.

In spite of all the suffering the Germans caused me and my family, I still feel attached to their history and culture, which I absorbed through my parents. I have done my best to recreate links with decent Germans.

In the sixties, contrary to the then-current policy of refusing any kind of contact, I advocated welcoming German youngsters into our neighborhood as volunteers, hosting them in local families, and making them aware of recent history. We established friendships with these volunteers, and now we visit them, and they visit us. We maintain an ongoing dialogue and do what we can to strengthen positive, anti-Fascist elements in Europe who protest and fight the resurgence of reactionary movements there.

Naturally, we can never forget the six million Jews – including 1.5 million innocent children – who were tortured and exterminated by the Nazis and their helpers. We may be able to reconcile ourselves with present-day Germany, but how can we forget that in the darkest hours of history, in our time of deepest despair, we were left alone to suffer and die, without any help from the so-called world powers? Even if we forgive those who live in Germany today, what about those who actively maimed and killed Jews and other victims of Nazi hatred?

If forgiving means renouncing blind hatred and feelings of revenge – yes, then it is possible. But does that require pardoning the monsters who committed the worst atrocities in human memory?

I may forgive those who stood by helplessly, and those who did not dare to speak up. I know how much courage it takes to stand up to authority and to oppose the kind of terror the Nazis imposed. But I also know that thousands of righteous people took the risk of helping and hiding Jews, knowing full well they were endangering themselves and their families.

Is it possible to forgive Hitler and his henchmen, his SS commanders and soldiers, his death-camp guards, his Gestapo officials? Is it possible to forgive torturers and murderers who starved, machine-gunned, and gassed hundreds of thousands of helpless men, women, and children?

I can forgive soldiers who fought against us in wars, even if they were wrongly motivated…I can forgive people who fight to protect themselves or to reclaim their rights, even if they are misled. But are there no limits to forgiveness?

Joel's understandable refusal to forgive the Nazis who cold-heartedly exterminated six million Jewish men, women and children is, I think, not motivated by bitterness or resentment, but by a fear that forgiveness would somehow be the same as exonerating them for their actions. As someone firmly committed to ensuring that similar atrocities can never happen again in the future, Joel cannot bring himself to forgive if that means pretending that the Holocaust never happened, or that the men who were responsible did not commit acts of deliberate, callous evil.

It would, of course, be deeply offensive to everyone who lost family and friends in the death camps to suggest that the Nazis' evil actions could be excused, or that they should not squarely shoulder the blame. It would also, I think, be entirely immoral. But forgiveness is not about excusing people or exonerating them from blame.

C. S. Lewis, writing in 1947 when the full horrors of the Holocaust had only just come to light, was well aware of the dangers of making excuses for people's evil acts. Yet he wrote, "There is all the difference in the world between forgiving and excusing." Most people, he suggested, don't like to admit when they've done something wrong, so they make excuses for their actions. Instead of asking for forgiveness, they try to get other people to accept their excuses and "extenuating circumstances," and to agree with them that they weren't really to blame. But, said Lewis, "If one was not really to blame then there is nothing to forgive. In that sense forgiveness and excusing are almost opposites."

> Real forgiveness means looking steadily at the sin, the sin that is left over without any excuse, after all allowances have been made, and seeing it in all its horror, dirt, meanness and malice, and nevertheless being wholly reconciled to the person who has done it. That, and only that, is forgiveness.[11]

BILL CHADWICK of Baton Rouge, Louisiana, makes
this distinction between forgiving and excusing quite
clearly in writing about the death of his son, Michael.
Never tempted simply to excuse the boy responsible for
Michael's death, Bill felt a compelling need to see justice
done. In the end, however, he discovered that justice by
itself couldn't bring him the satisfaction and peace he was
looking for:

> My twenty-one-year-old son Michael was killed in-
> stantly on October 23, 1993, in a car crash. His best
> friend, who was in the back seat, was also killed. The
> driver, who had been drinking heavily and was speed-
> ing recklessly, received minor injuries; he was subse-
> quently charged with two counts of vehicular homi-
> cide. Michael had only a trace of alcohol in his system,
> and his best friend had none.
>
> The wheels of justice grind very slowly. The courts
> took more than a year to find the case against the
> driver. We attended hearing after hearing, and each
> time the case was delayed. There was even an attempt
> by the defense attorney to discredit the findings of the
> blood-alcohol tests, although this was unsuccessful.
> Finally, the defendant pleaded guilty and was sent-
> enced to six years per count, to be served concurrently.
>
> We suggested to the probation office that a boot-
> camp-style program might be of benefit to him – we
> really weren't out to hurt him, but we believed he
> needed to pay for what he had done. All the same, we
> received a pretty ugly letter from his mother suggesting
> that we had somehow pushed for the maximum sen-

tence. She said that if it had been her son who died, with Michael driving, she would not have held a grudge. I suggested that until her son were actually dead, she should not talk

Bill and Michael Chadwick, 1993

about what she would or wouldn't do.

Her son was finally sentenced to six months in boot-camp, with the rest of his six-year sentence to be served on intensive parole. In six months, her son was coming home. Ours was not.

I guess I had bought into the belief that, somehow, things would be different after the driver had been brought to justice. I think that is what people mean when they talk about "getting closure." We think that if there is someone to blame, then we can put the matter to rest. It's sort of like thinking that if it somehow makes sense, or if the victims get some sort of justice, then the pain will finally go away. In the years since Michael's death, I have read countless accounts of bereaved people who are looking for closure of this sort. I have even seen them on the Oprah Winfrey show, shouting for the death penalty, as if having the perpetrator dead would somehow help.

I was angry at the driver, of course. But I was angry at Michael, too. After all, he had made some really bad decisions that night; he had put his life in jeopardy. I had to go through this anger in order to come to grips with my feelings. However, even after the sentencing, I did not find closure. What I did find was the same big hole in my soul – and nothing to fill it with.

It was some months later that it hit me: until I could forgive the driver, I would not get the closure I was looking for. Forgiving is different from removing responsibility. The driver was still responsible for Michael's death, but I had to forgive him before I could let the incident go. No amount of punishment could ever even the score. I had to be willing to forgive without the score being even. And this process of forgiveness did not really involve the driver – it involved me. It was a process that I had to go through; I had to change, no matter what he did.

The road to forgiveness was long and painful. I had to forgive more than just the driver. I had to forgive Michael, and God (for allowing it to happen), and myself. Ultimately, it was my inability to forgive myself that was the most difficult. There were many times in my own life I had driven Michael places when I myself was under the influence of alcohol. But that was the key to my forgiveness – to forgive myself. My anger at other people was just my own fear turned outward. I had projected my own guilt onto others – the driver, the courts, God, Michael – so that I would not have to look at myself. And it wasn't until I could see my part in this that my outlook could change.

This is what I learned: that the closure we seek comes in forgiving. And this closure is really up to us, because the power to forgive lies not outside us, but within our own souls.

Michael's father learned what may be the most painful lesson for any parent. Yet it is one that each of us needs to learn, whatever our situation in life. Unless we have forgiveness in our hearts toward those who harm us, we will find no peace, however "right" we may be in claiming retribution.

In a society that places a premium on revenge, this is hardly a popular idea. Increasingly, sentencing by a court is no longer enough; people want a personal role in the act of retribution. Several states have even introduced legislation that gives murder victims' families the right to be present at executions. Yet these families never seem to find the peace they are looking for. Their desire to see others hurt by the same violence that has hurt them is never satisfied. Instead of healing their wounds, their quest for revenge leaves them disillusioned and angry.

Forgiving is not condoning. In some cases, "forgiving and forgetting" is not only impossible, but immoral. How can anyone forget a child? Pain, indignation and anger are perfectly understandable, and perhaps even necessary, but ultimately these must yield to a longing for reconciliation.

6 Forgiveness when Reconciliation is Impossible

IT MAY BE INFINITELY WORSE to refuse to forgive
than to murder, because the latter may be an impulse of a
moment of heat, whereas the former is a cold and deliberate choice of the heart.

George Macdonald

WHEN MARIETTA JAEGER'S seven-year-old
daughter was kidnapped from their tent during a camping
trip in Montana, her initial reaction was one of rage:

I was seething with hate, ravaged with a desire for revenge. "Even if Susie were brought back alive and well

this minute, I could kill that man for what he has done to my family," I said to my husband, and I meant it with every fiber of my being.

Justifiable as her reaction was, Marietta says she soon realized that no amount of anger could bring her daughter back. She was not ready to forgive her daughter's kidnapper: for a long time she told herself that to do so would be to betray her daughter and condone the kidnapper's actions. Yet deep down inside, she sensed that forgiving him was the only way she would ever be able to cope with her loss.

In desperation, she began praying, not only for her daughter's safe return, but also for the kidnapper. Over the weeks and months that followed, her prayers for Susie's return became harder and harder; but strangely, her prayers for the kidnapper became easier and more earnest. She simply had to find the person who had taken away her beloved child. And she even felt an uncanny desire to talk with him face to face.

Then one night, a year to the minute after her daughter had been abducted, Marietta received a phone call. It was the kidnapper. Marietta was afraid – the voice was smug and taunting – but she was surprised at her genuine feeling of compassion for the man at the other end of the line. And she noticed that, as she calmed down, he did too. They talked for over an hour.

Luckily Marietta was able to record their conversation. Even so, it was months before the FBI finally tracked him down and arrested him, and it was only then that she knew

Marietta and Susie Jaeger, the day before Susie was kidnapped

for certain that Susie would never be coming home. The investigators had found the backbone of a small child among the kidnapper's belongings.

State law offered the death penalty, but Marietta was not out for revenge. She writes: "By then, I had finally come to learn that justice is not about punishment, but restoration." She requested instead that Susie's killer be given an alternative sentence of life imprisonment with psychiatric counseling. The tormented young man committed suicide, but she never regretted her decision to offer him help. And her efforts at peacemaking did not end there. Today, she is part of a group that works for reconciliation between murderers and the families of victims. It is part of her healing process, and theirs.

As Marietta's experience shows, not all stories have tidy endings. Even when we are able to confront the person we need to forgive, they may not be the least bit sorry for their actions. Sometimes a murderer is never apprehended, or a marriage partner runs away, never to be seen again. Is forgiveness still possible?

UNABLE TO COPE with the senseless murder of his sister, Frances, Daniel Coleman eventually took his own life. This double tragedy changed the life of their mother, Anne. Today she counsels men on Delaware's death row. Her work began when she first met Barbara Lewis, a woman whose son was on death row. After visiting Barbara's son together, they began to visit other inmates as well:

> That's how I met Billy. He'd had no visitors, and he was very lonely. I cry when I think of how he was hanged; how they made him stand on the gallows in that howling wind for at least fifteen minutes while they waited for the witnesses to arrive. After his execution I thought I couldn't go on.
>
> Then I got to know a little boy called Marcus. His father is also on death row. He has no mother and has lost both of his sisters, and he has nightmares because now he's going to lose his father, too.
>
> I know that hating someone is not going to bring my daughter back. And at this point, I don't know if I'll ever find the person who killed her, anyway. But one has to find healing somehow, and I've found it by helping the Barbaras and Marcuses of this world. Helping them has given me more healing than I ever imagined.

JENNIFER, a long-time acquaintance, lost her fiancé when he left her ten days before their wedding date, and she never saw him again. They had been engaged for more than a year, and although the relationship had occasionally faltered, she was sure that this time everything was going to work out. She was deeply in love, and very excited. She had finally graduated from nursing school, and her wedding dress was nearly finished. Then everything fell apart:

> My fiancé revealed that he had been dishonest with me – there were things in his past that were still an obstacle to our marriage. To make things worse, he wanted to run away from it all rather than confront his past. I was shattered. I wept for days and was heartbroken for years. I blamed myself for his dishonesty, and I became bitter.

Thirty years later, Jennifer is still single, but she is no longer bitter. Even though she cannot tell him, she has genuinely and entirely forgiven her fiancé. And although she sometimes still aches for the marriage that never was and the love she lost, she has found real fulfillment in helping and serving other people – the old and the sick, expectant mothers and disabled children. Few of her friends know about her past. Happy and energetic, she is too busy to entertain self-pity:

> Because I am single, I can do things a busy wife and mother could never do. I can give of myself whenever and wherever I am needed. And I have cared for and loved more children than I ever could have otherwise.

JULIE LEFT THE BRUDERHOF community, together with her husband and children, after she confronted her husband for molesting their daughter. In spite of her shock and horror at what he had done, she still loved him and hoped that away from the community they could rebuild their relationship as a family. Sadly, things didn't work out that way.

> I was foundering on the verge of desperation. My husband had become a stranger to me, and I could no longer live with him in what had become a hell. We spent a year away from the community, hoping to save our marriage and our family, but it was no use. Everything was lost.
>
> I left him and returned to the Bruderhof, angry, hurt, hateful, rejected, despairing, outraged, humiliated – even this long string of adjectives cannot express what I felt. A battle raged in my heart. I wanted to forgive, but I also wanted to lash out in revenge, and every time I thought of his new wife (he had divorced me and re-married), it rekindled my emotions. It has not been an easy battle, and it continues still, as I witness the effect of the abuse and the break-up on our five children.
>
> Wanting to forgive – this was my battle: genuinely wanting to forgive him. I knew this should be my response. But how could I, when he showed so little remorse? And what would be the practical expression of my forgiveness?
>
> I didn't want to gloss over what he had done in any way and I let him know that I could not allow my children to stay with him any longer. But I decided that the most constructive thing I could do was to accept the divorce.

I have since discovered that forgiving him was not a one-time thing. I must affirm my forgiveness again and again. Sometimes I doubt that I have ever forgiven him at all, and I have to battle through that, too. But I know that, ultimately, the wrongs my husband has done to me cannot destroy me.

Julie's story illustrates a vital point: even if her former husband never shows remorse, she still has to forgive him. If she does not, she will remain bound to him by her bitterness, and he will continue to influence her thoughts and emotions. She will remain wounded by what he did to her and her children for the rest of her life. Yet by letting go of her anger and hatred, by realizing that bitterness is wasted energy, she has found new strength to love her children and move on.

7 Forgiveness in Everyday Life

LOOKING DOWN into my father's
dead face
for the last time
my mother said without
tears, without smiles
but with *civility,*
"Good night, Willie Lee, I'll see you
in the morning."
And it was then I knew the healing
of all our wounds
is forgiveness
that permits a promise
of our return
at the end.

Alice Walker

MANY OF US WILL NEVER be faced with forgiving a murderer or rapist. But all of us are faced daily with the need to forgive a partner, child, friend or colleague – perhaps dozens of times in a single day. And this task is no less important.

In his poem, "A Poison Tree," William Blake shows how the smallest resentment can blossom and bear deadly fruit:

> I was angry with my friend:
> I told my wrath, my wrath did end.
> I was angry with my foe:
> I told it not, my wrath did grow.
>
> And I water'd it in fears,
> Night and morning with my tears;
> And I sunned it with smiles,
> And with soft deceitful wiles.
>
> And it grew both day and night,
> Till it bore an apple bright;
> And my foe beheld it shine,
> And he knew that it was mine,
>
> And into my garden stole
> When the night had veil'd the pole:
> In the morning glad I see
> My foe outstretched beneath the tree.

The petty grudges of everyday life are the seeds to Blake's tree. If they fall into fertile hearts, they will grow, and if they are tended and nurtured they will take on a life of their own. They may be small, seemingly insignificant, hardly noticeable at first, but they must nonetheless be overcome. Blake shows us in the first two lines how easily this can be done: we must face our anger immediately and root it out before it grows.

I had to learn not to hold on to grudges early in my life. My childhood was a happy one for the most part, but I had my share of unpleasant experiences. I was a sickly child. Soon after I was born the doctors told my mother that I had hydrocephalus ("water on the brain") and would never walk. Even though this did not prove to be true – I started walking at two-and-a-half – the nickname "water-head" stuck. This hurt my parents the most, but it affected me as well.

I was lonely. There were seven children in our family, but I was the only boy. In addition, my father was gone for three of the first five years of my life. So I longed for friends.

When I was six, I had to have a large tumor removed from my leg. This was the first of many such operations over the next three decades. The surgery lasted two hours, and the threat of infection – this was before the days of antibiotics, and we were living in the backwoods of Para-guay – hung over me for days. After my leg was stitched shut, I walked home from the hospital. No one offered me crutches, let alone a wagon. I can still see my father's shocked face as I limped into our house, though he didn't say a thing.

That was typical of my parents. We never heard them speak ill of others, and they did not allow us to, either. Like any other parents, they struggled with their feelings when they felt that one of us children had been mistreated by a teacher or other adults. But they insisted that the only way to overcome the little indignities of life was to forgive.

When I was fourteen, we moved to the United States. The change from a village in the South American wilderness to a public high school in New York was enormous. The English language was certainly a barrier for me, but I was also shy because I felt I was awkward and clumsy. Every child wants to be recognized by his or her peers – no one wants to be left behind – and I was no different. I desperately wanted to be accepted, and I went out of my way to please my new classmates. At first I was spurned, especially by one boy who had the reputation of being a bully. Then I began to fight back. My friends were all immigrants like myself, and we mocked him mercilessly, speaking German among ourselves because we knew he didn't understand a word of it. Our animosity led to more than a few bloody noses.

In my twenties, I again had to deal with feelings of rejection. My relationship with a young woman deepened and we became engaged, but then one day she suddenly turned her back on me. It was a struggle to forgive her, and also to forgive myself, especially since I had no idea why she had ended the relationship. (I convinced myself that it was my fault that things had gone wrong, because I felt I was such an awkward misfit.) A few years later, my hopes were dashed for a second time, when another woman, too, broke off our relationship after several months. My world crashed around me as I tried to make sense of what had happened. What had I done wrong?

It took me a long time to get over my hurt and rebuild my confidence. But my father assured me that in time I would find the right person, and this proved to be true when some years later I found my wife, Verena.

IT IS LESS DIFFICULT to forgive a stranger than a person we know and trust. This is why it is so hard to overcome betrayal by close friends or colleagues. They know our deepest thoughts, our frailties, our quirks – and when they turn on us, we are left reeling.

Pete, a friend from Virginia, had just such an experience:

Before moving to another state and leaving my business, I had to settle affairs with my partner of ten years. This was complicated by the fact that he and his wife were very close to me; we had been friends for the past fifteen years.

No one would advise me about how best to make an equitable settlement of our business assets. I wanted to be not just fair, but generous. I wanted nothing hanging on my conscience. So I came up with a division that would give me half of the earnings to the date I left, and leave them with the other half, the jobs in progress, and the equity and good will of the business with which to continue. But they saw the whole thing differently and stopped talking to me the day I gave notice. Unfortunately, I had given two months' notice, so the transition was long, silent, and lonely, punctuated only by angry words.

We still had not signed an agreement by the time I left. Lawyers had been brought in by both of us, but they only clouded the waters. I had wanted an outside source to arbitrate the offer, but they fired the arbitrator and sought advice instead from an accountant we had worked with for seven years. I'm not sure just what happened, but he quickly lost his objectivity and began to work against me.

It took a lot of offers and counter-offers finally to come to an agreement. They insisted that even though I was to be paid off by December, they would not be able to mail the check until December 31. Only later did I learn that this delay made me liable for one-half of our earnings for the entire year – even though I had only received my share of the earnings through to June. I ended up paying $50,000 in taxes. I was so angry I could not sleep for days. I felt totally betrayed by my friend and the accountant. I felt they had conspired to crush me.

I really had to reach deep to forgive that one, but I somehow found the strength to do so. Then I realized that I needed to write and ask their forgiveness, too. I felt such a release as I licked the envelope and put the letter in the mail. No matter what their answer, I needed to be free of my anger.

About a month later, a friend of mine who had advised me to forgive called to ask if I had been able to do so. I told her that I had, and she answered, "I thought so; I've noticed a real freeing in him, too."

UNFORTUNATELY, betrayal by friends or colleagues is common in all circles. As a pastor in the Bruderhof community, my father was known and respected for his ability to give encouragement and good advice. Wherever he went, people wanted to talk to him. Many had things they needed to get off their chest; others just needed a listening ear. But the very things that made some people like him made others envy him.

Papa had suffered from kidney problems around the time I was born, and as he grew older these problems became worse. Life in Paraguay was harsh; disease was rampant, and the fight to survive was made harder by tensions in our community. The burden of Papa's leadership responsibilities weighed on him as never before. At one point, after several weeks of steady physical decline, his doctors told him he had only forty hours to live. Fearing the worst, he summoned the entire community to his bedside, encouraging them to be strong and steadfast in the harsh conditions. He also passed on his responsibilities as leader to three men, one of them his brother-in-law.

As it turned out, Papa miraculously recovered, but rather than handing back the reins, the community's new leaders told him that his leadership days were over: the doctor had declared him too weak to continue such demanding work. The main reason, they said, was the "emotional instability" he had displayed at the height of his illness, when he had had bizarre dreams and hallucinations.

Never the kind of leader who was prepared simply to impose his will on others, Papa decided not to fight the decision and began to work in our small missionary school and hospital.

Though my parents did not realize it at the time, this turn of events was no accident. It had been calculated in a deliberate attempt to bar him from his life's work. In fact, the doctor had suggested only a few weeks of additional rest, but his words had been twisted by the new leaders for their own ends. (It was only thirty years later that another doctor discovered and explained to him the real reason for his hallucinations – they were a side-effect of the primitive bromide medications used to treat him.) Never once, however, did we children sense any bitterness on his part.

It wasn't long, however, before new problems surfaced within our community. Concerned that genuine compassion was being squeezed out by rules and regulations, my parents joined a handful of other members in trying to raise a voice of warning, but their words were misunderstood. Accused of deliberately trying to split the community, several of them, including Papa, were sent away. Although a skilled gardener (he had studied horticulture in Zurich), he was unable to find work of any kind. Paraguay's German settlers, who tended to be sympathetic to the Nazis, looked on him with suspicion, and British and American expatriates feared him simply because he was German. Finally, he found employment as a farm manager in a leper colony.

In the early 1940s, no cure existed for leprosy, and such work was extremely dangerous. He was warned of conta-

Heinrich and Annemarie Arnold, 1958

gion, and was told by more than one doctor that he might never see his wife or children again. The anguish he suffered is hard to describe.

I will never forget my excitement the day Papa returned from the leper colony. Straddling his shoulders as he strode toward the house, I called out, "Papa is home!" to every passer-by. For the most part, we were met with icy stares.

It was years before I found out the real reason for Papa's expulsion: he had felt that the leaders of our community were becoming too autocratic, repressive, and cold-hearted. When he had pleaded with them for more compassion and understanding, they had accused him of "emotionalism." Papa still did not become bitter, however.

I was in my twenties by the time I first heard these stories from my father's old friends. I was horrified. How would I react, I wondered, if I were pushed aside by trusted friends and colleagues without explanation?

In 1980 I found out. My community suddenly asked me to step down from my role as a leader, a job I had held for almost ten years. To this day I am not completely sure why it happened. Certainly there was an element of the same divisive jealousy that had hurt my parents forty years earlier, but this time it was my friends, colleagues and siblings who for the most part turned against me. All of a sudden, the very same people who had always praised and encouraged me began to find fault with everything I had ever done.

Confused and angry, I was tempted to fight back. The move had come at a very bad time for me: my mother had died of cancer only a few weeks before, and as far as I could tell the community needed me more than ever. I desperately wanted to set my record straight and re-establish my "rightful" place. Papa, however, refused to support my fight back. He reminded me that, in the end, we are not responsible for what others do to us – only for what we do to them.

As we talked, I began to realize I wasn't as pure and blameless as I had thought. Deep down, I held grudges against certain members of my community. Instead of trying to justify myself, I needed to ask for forgiveness. As soon as I did, my struggle took on a wholly new meaning. I felt as if a dam had burst open somewhere deep down inside my heart. All I had felt before was the pain of hurt pride; now I could afford to ask myself: What does it matter in the long run?

With a new determination to set things straight and
take the blame for whatever tensions existed, I went with
my wife to people we felt we had hurt in the past and
asked them to forgive us. As we went from one to another,
we felt our hearts become lighter.

That year was a very painful one for me and my wife,
but it was also an important one. It prepared us for the
responsibilities we now carry by giving us a greater sense
of compassion for others. And it taught us some lessons
we will never forget. First, it doesn't matter if people misunderstand you or accuse you unjustly; what matters is
that you don't misunderstand others or accuse them unjustly. Second, though the decision to forgive must always
come from within, we cannot change in our own strength.
The power of forgiveness comes not from us, but from our
own experience of being forgiven.

JIM AND CAROLYN WEEKS went through hard times
the same year. They, too, found that forgiveness is the only
way to reconciliation. Carolyn writes:

> In 1980 we had already been living with the Bruderhof
> for five years, and we wanted to become full members.
> But it was a time of chaos and uncertainty, and when we
> couldn't understand things, we easily became upset and
> ended up backing ourselves into a corner.
>
> Finally we decided to ask for a few weeks' leave from
> the community so that we could work things out on our

own and find peace. Unfortunately, our request was misunderstood, and we ended up leaving the community as if for good. I will never forget driving away. Some of our friends came out to say good-bye, but all I could feel inside was a great emptiness.

Only weeks before we had been certain we would soon be permanent members of the Bruderhof, and now all our dreams were shattered. We had sacrificed everything to join this way of life. As a young married couple we had come with some of our wedding gifts still wrapped. We had given the community our car and everything else we owned.

The Bruderhof provided us with a truckload of furniture, and even a driver to carry us to our new home in Baltimore, yet we still struggled with feelings of abandonment and rejection. We felt as though we were miserable failures. We tried to block out all our memories – there had been many happy times – and threw ourselves into our new life.

It took us eight years to recover financially, with plenty of help from family and friends. By this time we had come to accept our lot. Both of us had secure jobs, the kids were enrolled in good schools with plenty of friends, and we were only a few years away from paying off our mortgage. But inside we were empty and lonely, and we knew something was missing. Initially, we had talked about trying to return to the Bruderhof, but after a few years we gave up on this hope completely. We didn't realize it, but we had built up a great wall of bitterness in our hearts.

Then one morning, about ten years after we had left, the phone rang just as our kids were getting on the school bus. It was a couple from the Bruderhof who were in town and wanted to see us. At first we were apprehensive, but we invited them for dinner. Even though we hadn't sorted out all of our feelings, we knew we had been deeply hurt. The couple left, and we didn't see anyone from the Bruderhof again until several months later, when we visited "just for one weekend."

Jim and Carolyn Weeks with their daughter Veronica, 1983

We ended up coming back for a second weekend, and we were invited to a special members' meeting to explain our position and to set the record straight, so that at least we could be friends again. The meeting started out fine, but by the end of it we realized to our great shock that the person we had trusted the most had in fact understood us the least. That hurt. After that meeting, we were still willing to be friends with the community, but no more than that.

Imagine our surprise, then, when the next morning this man and his wife drove two hours to see us, to ask us for our forgiveness. When we heard that they had come, we didn't want to see them at first; we were too afraid of what we might say. Then we reluctantly agreed to talk to them. To our amazement, they met us with open arms and eyes filled with tears. They said they were sorry and held out their hands as a greeting of peace. What a moment! After all they had done to us, after ten years of nightmares, after all we had been through, how could we ever start again? We wanted to hold back, but we couldn't. Our hands went out to theirs and we forgave them…Within months we were back with the Bruderhof.

Once Jim and Carolyn returned home, it wasn't long before they began to see that they, too, were not without guilt. Carolyn writes:

> We had to see that there were two sides to the story – that we had been obstinate and opinionated. Our pride was an obstacle to reconciliation.

Very few disputes are one-sided. In our pride, however, we see only the faults of others and are blind to our own faults. Unless we are able to learn a little humility, we cannot forgive or be forgiven. This is painful, but it is an inevitable and inescapable part of life. Forgiveness allows us to move beyond pain, even as we acknowledge it, to the joy that comes from love. M. Scott Peck writes:

> There is no way that we can live a rich life unless we are willing to suffer repeatedly, experiencing depression and despair, fear and anxiety, grief and sadness, anger and the agony of forgiving, confusion and doubt, criticism and rejection. A life lacking these emotional upheavals will not only be useless to ourselves; it will be useless to others. We cannot heal without being willing to be hurt.[12]

True community – with family, friends or colleagues – demands that we bare our souls to each other. C. S. Lewis goes so far as to say that "to love at all is to be vulnerable. The only place outside Heaven where you can be perfectly safe from all the dangers and perturbations of love is Hell."[13]

Jim and Carolyn's story shows plainly, however, that forgiveness can bring people back together. Hard times, if overcome, can lead to greater love. They can strengthen rather than weaken the bond of unity.

8 Forgiveness in Marriage

PEOPLE ASK ME what advice I have for a married couple struggling in their relationship. I always answer: pray and forgive. And to young people from violent homes, I say: pray and forgive. And again, even to the single mother with no family support: pray and forgive.

Mother Teresa

OVER MANY YEARS of marriage counseling, I have seen again and again that unless a husband and wife forgive each other daily, marriage can become a living hell. I have also seen that the thorniest problems can often be resolved with three simple words: I am sorry.

To ask one's partner for forgiveness can be difficult. It requires humility and the acknowledgment of weaknesses and failures. And yet this is what makes a marriage healthy: both partners living in mutual humility, fully aware of their inner dependence on each other.

Dietrich Bonhoeffer, the famed German pastor imprisoned by Hitler in the 1930s for his opposition to the Nazi regime, used to tell the members of the small community he founded about the need to "live together in forgiveness," because without forgiveness no human fellowship – least of all a marriage – can survive: "Don't insist on your rights," he once wrote. "Don't blame each other, don't judge or condemn each other, don't find fault with each other, but accept each other as you are, and forgive each other every day from the bottom of your hearts."[14]

In thirty-one years of marriage, Verena and I have had no lack of opportunities to test our willingness to forgive. Only a week after our wedding we had our first crisis. My sister, an artist, had made us a beautiful set of dishes. We had invited my parents and sisters over to dinner in our new apartment, and Verena had spent all afternoon cooking. I set the table with my sister's crockery. My family arrived and we sat down to eat. Suddenly both ends of the table collapsed – I had not snapped the hinged extensions properly into place. Food and broken pottery covered the floor, and my wife fled the room in tears. It was hours before she could forgive me and we could laugh about this disaster, though it has now become a family legend.

By the time we had eight children, there were plenty of reasons for disagreement. Every evening, Verena would bathe the children and dress them in clean pajamas, and they would wait for me on the sofa with their favorite

books. When I came home from work, however, they
wanted to play, and sometimes we ended up romping in
the yard. Verena still remembers the hours she spent removing grass stains and mud – and not without a little
grumbling!

Most of our children suffered from asthma, and when
they were small they woke us almost nightly with their
coughing and wheezing. This, too, brought discord between us, especially when she reminded me that I could
get out of bed and attend to them just as well as she.

We had plenty of arguments over my work as well.
As a salesman for our publishing house, I spent countless
days on the road. And because my territory covered western New York – Buffalo, Rochester and Syracuse – I was
often a good six or eight hours' drive away from home.
Later, as a community leader, I had to make frequent trips
to Canada, Europe and even Africa. I always ended up
defending such trips as "vitally important," though this
assertion did little to soothe my wife, who packed my suit-
cases, adjusted herself to a hectic schedule, and often
stayed behind with the children.

Then there was the *New York Times*. After a hard day on
the road, I couldn't see the harm in stretching out with the
paper for a few minutes while the children played happily
around me, and I voiced this opinion rather vehemently.
Only later did I come to see my selfishness.

I often think about how our marriage might have
turned out if we hadn't learned to forgive each other on
a daily basis right from the start. So many couples sleep

in the same bed and share the same house but remain miles apart inwardly because they have built up a wall of resentment between themselves. The bricks in this wall may be very small – a forgotten anniversary, a misunderstanding, a business meeting that took precedence over a long-awaited family outing. But the resulting division they create can spell disaster.

Many marriages could be saved by the simple realization that people are imperfect. Too often, couples assume that a "good" relationship is one that is free from arguments and disagreements. Unable to live up to this unrealistic expectation, they become disillusioned; before long, they separate on the grounds of "incompatibility."

Human imperfection means that we will make mistakes and hurt each other, unknowingly and even knowingly. In my own life, the only fail-safe solution I have found is to forgive, seventy times a day if necessary. C. S. Lewis writes:

> To forgive the incessant provocations of daily life – to keep on forgiving the bossy mother-in-law, the bullying husband, the nagging wife, the selfish daughter, the deceitful son – how can we do it? Only, I think, by remembering where we stand, by meaning our words when we say in our prayers each night, "Forgive our trespasses as we forgive those who trespass against us."[15]

THE POWER OF FORGIVENESS is wonderfully illustrated by the story of my wife's parents, Hans and Margrit Meier. Hans was a strong-willed man, and his stubbornness caused more than one period of separation in their marriage. An ardent anti-militarist, he was imprisoned only months after their wedding in 1929 because he refused to join the Swiss army.

Shortly after his release, the couple was separated again. Margrit had discovered the Bruderhof and wanted to join our community. Hans, a religious socialist with very different ideas about communal life, did not. Margrit had recently given birth to their first child, and she begged him to join them, but Hans would not be easily swayed. It was several months before she convinced him to come.

Thirty years and eleven children later, they separated again. By this time they were living in South America; it was 1961, a time of great internal confusion and upheaval for the Bruderhof. Unable to see his own failures – or to forgive those of others – Hans became estranged both from his wife and from the community. Margrit and the children moved to the United States. Hans dug in his heels and settled in Buenos Aires, where he remained for the next eleven years.

There were no signs of outward rancor, but there were no signs of healing either. Slowly, a wall of bitterness rose up which threatened to keep them apart forever. When I married Verena in 1966, Hans did not even attend the wedding, and our children began to grow up without a grandfather on their mother's side.

In 1972 I went to Buenos Aires with Verena's brother, Andreas, in an attempt to find some kind of reconciliation with Hans, but he wasn't interested – at least not at first. He only wanted to recount his side of the story and let us

Hans and Margrit Meier on their 50th wedding anniversary, May 11, 1977

know, once again, how many times he had been hurt. On the last day of our trip, though, something changed. He announced that he would visit us in the United States. He insisted that he would come for just two weeks, and emphasized the fact that he had a return ticket. But it was a start.

When the visit finally materialized, we were disappointed. Hans simply could not forgive. We made every effort to clear up past difficulties and acknowledged our guilt in the events leading up to his long estrangement, but we weren't getting anywhere. Intellectually, Hans knew that the only thing standing between us was his inability to forgive. Yet he could not bring himself to do it.

Then came the turning point. In the middle of a community meeting, my uncle Hans-Hermann, who was dying of lung cancer, summoned all his strength, walked up to Hans, and tapped him on the chest saying, "Hans, the change must happen here!" These words cost a tremendous effort: Hans-Hermann was receiving supplemental oxygen through nasal tubes and was barely able to speak. Hans was completely disarmed. His coldness melted away, and he decided there and then to forgive – and return. After traveling back to Argentina to wind up his affairs, he moved back to join Margrit and the community and soon proved to be the same dedicated, energetic member he had been decades before.

In all his years away, Hans had never touched another woman. During the same long decade, Margrit had prayed daily for her husband's return. All the same, both had been hurt, and it took a long time for them fully to rebuild their trust in one another. As their son-in-law, I can testify that they did: they lived in love and joy with each other and their children, grandchildren, and great-grandchildren until Margrit's death sixteen years later.

Even if we forgive someone who has truly hurt us, isn't it only natural to remain indignant at what they have done? This is a difficult question, but perhaps it has more to do with our difficulty in upholding a human sense of justice than with forgiving. As Hans and Margrit discovered, forgiveness is more than justice. It is a gift. And to those who cannot accept it, it may seem irrational or stupid.

The story of my parents-in-law shows that even long separations can be healed. But can a marriage damaged by adultery or abuse ever be fully repaired? It's easy to say no, but in my experience most people can change, given enough time, motivation, and support. Love reconciles and forgives. Even if circumstances dictate a temporary separation, faithful love is the only way to healing and reunion. Those who divorce and then remarry close the door to future chances of reconciliation.

THE ENORMOUS BREACH of trust caused by infidelity can, of course, take years to heal. At first it may be necessary for a couple to live separately, receiving professional counseling, or less formal help, under the guidance of someone they both trust. They must be willing to work toward rebuilding their trust so that the marriage can be restored.

When I began writing this book, I had just begun counseling a couple whose marriage was destroyed by adultery. Ed and Carol were married nine years ago. Even before he was married, Ed had been a problem drinker, and this brought great tensions to the marriage from the start. Although they remained together in the same house, inwardly they drifted further and further apart. Some years into their marriage, Ed began a secret affair with a neighbor. Carol found herself becoming more and more depressed, though she never knew why.

Ed and Carol first came to the Bruderhof in the mid-1990s. Within days Ed had told his wife about his affair. His guilty conscience gave him no peace, and he found himself unable to contain his secret any longer. Carol was totally dumbfounded. She had sensed for a long time that something was wrong, but she had never imagined such deception. Justifiably angry, she told Ed that their marriage was over, and that she could never forgive him.

It wasn't hard to sympathize with her emotions, but I knew from the start that if she couldn't forgive Ed, the deep wounds he had inflicted on her would never be healed. I suggested to her that accepting defeat would only drive them further apart and rule out the possibility of them ever coming back together again.

At the same time, though, I advised an immediate separation with counseling for both partners. Such a separation would help both Ed and Carol come to terms with their emotions on their own. There could be no "quick fix," and the process would be long and painful. A new relationship had to be built from the bottom up.

Ed and Carol were separated for several months, but during this period both of them made remarkable progress in their relationship. At first they communicated by phone calls only. Later their conversations grew longer and more relaxed, and they began to visit each other as well. Ed stopped drinking, and slowly the joy and freedom that follow an admission of guilt began to replace the agony of months of soul-searching. Carol struggled with plenty of hard moments, but she was eager to start over – not just for the sake of the children, who had stayed with her when Ed moved out of the house, but for her own sake as well.

She began to feel a new love for Ed. Most important, she was willing to forgive him fully. Once she recognized that she herself was not entirely blameless in the matter of their estrangement, she was able to meet Ed on his level.

Now, ten months later, Ed and Carol are together again. In a special service held to celebrate the re-founding of their marriage, their mutual forgiveness was publicly affirmed. Then, faces beaming, they exchanged new rings.

Ed and Carol are not the first couple I have counseled through the heartache of adultery, and they may not be the last. Yet I am confident that other couples, too, will find strength to weather even this storm, as long as both partners are willing to seek renewal on the basis of mutual forgiveness and love.

9 Forgiving an Abusive Parent

IT IS FREEING TO BECOME aware that we do not have to be victims of our past and can learn new ways of responding. But there is a step beyond this recognition… It is the step of forgiveness. Forgiveness is love practiced among people who love poorly. It sets us free without wanting anything in return.

Henri J. M. Nouwen

MANY PEOPLE TODAY struggle to find healing from a broken past. Countless lives have been deeply wounded by childhood abuse – psychological, physical, and, worst of all, sexual. Television shows and magazines deal with these themes on a daily basis. On one program after another, survivors pour out their painful stories to a jaded and uncaring public. Yet it seems that no amount of soul-baring brings them the healing they seek. How can they find it?

Ronald grew up on an Appalachian farmstead in western Pennsylvania. Forty or so family members shared the same house, trying to eke out a living from the land. His childhood was brutal: he tells of cousins who tried to hang one another and a grandmother who once fired at disobedient children with a shotgun full of rock salt.

Ronald's father was an intelligent man, though, and eventually left the farm with his children and moved to Long Island, where he found work. His finances improved, but his relationships did not. His wife left him, and he routinely beat his children, sometimes severely. Ronald lived in constant fear of the violence that awaited him each day when he returned home from school.

Then his father was badly injured in an automobile accident. His neck was broken, and he was paralyzed from the neck down. Once the tyrant of the household, he was now a paraplegic, utterly dependent on others to care for his daily needs.

As a young adult, Ronald had every reason to abandon his father. Why should he stay and care for the man who had ruined his life? Yet he has never left his father's side. Although medical and disability benefits provide some nursing help, he takes on most of his father's care himself. For years he has faithfully seen to his father's daily needs – washing, dressing, and exercising the lifeless limbs that once beat him mercilessly, sometimes to the point of unconsciousness. Often he takes him outdoors in his wheelchair, and they talk about the emotional battles they have both fought and are still fighting.

Demons of the past still haunt Ronald on occasion, but he says he has finally found a measure of the peace he so sorely missed in his childhood. More than anything else, his loving service attests to the forgiveness and healing both he and his father now feel.

KARL KEIDERLING, a member of the Bruderhof community who died in 1993, also suffered a harsh childhood. The only son of a German working-class family, his early years were clouded by the First World War and the economic devastation that followed it. His mother died when he was four and his stepmother when he was fourteen. After her death, his father put an ad in the paper that intentionally excluded Karl: "Widower with three daughters looking for a housekeeper; possibility of future marriage."

Several women applied, and in the end one decided to stay. It was only afterwards that she found out about the existence of a boy in the house, and she never quite forgave Karl's father for withholding this from her. Karl's food was always poorer than the rest of the family's, and she complained about him constantly.

Karl's father, for his part, was silent in the face of his new wife's stern, unfeeling manner and did nothing to defend his son. In fact, he joined her in mistreating the boy and often beat him with a leather strap mounted with

brass rings. When Karl tried to protect himself, his father would only
grow more furious and hit him over
the head and in the face.

Karl left home as soon as he
could. Attracted by the youth movement sweeping the country in those
postwar years, he joined ranks with
atheists and anarchists and others
who believed they had to change the
world, and set out to make sure that
society would never be the same

Karl Keiderling

again. He wandered through Germany until he came
across the Bruderhof, where he immediately felt at home,
and decided to stay. He threw himself vigorously into life
at the community, but his childhood experiences didn't
leave him. Again and again his resentment toward his parents hung like a heavy weight on his heart. Finally, he went
to my grandfather and poured out his anger and hatred.

The response was startling: my grandfather suggested
that Karl write to his parents and ask their forgiveness, to
set right the times when he had consciously hurt their
feelings or caused them grief. He told Karl to look only at
his own guilt, not at theirs. At first Karl was taken aback,
but eventually he took my grandfather's advice. His father
acknowledged his letter, and although he never apologized
for any of the terrible wrongs he had done, Karl's burden
was lifted. For the first time in his life he was able to find
peace, closing a painful chapter of his life, and he never
complained about his childhood again.

MARY, A FRIEND of our family's, overcame painful memories of abuse in a similar way:

> My mother died at the age of forty-two, leaving behind my father and eight children, aged one to nineteen. This loss was devastating for our family, and my father broke down emotionally just when we needed him most. He tried to molest my sister and me, so I began to resent his presence and hate him.
>
> He moved away, and I went off to school in Europe and didn't see him for another seven years. But I held on to my hatred, and it grew inside me.
>
> When I returned to South America, I fell in love with and became engaged to a childhood friend. My father asked to meet with me, but I refused. In no way did I want to meet him. My fiancé insisted. He said that I could not refuse such a meeting, and that I had to respond to his longing for reconciliation. It cost me a real battle, but in the end I agreed.
>
> We met my father in a café. Before I had said anything, he turned to me, broken, and asked for my forgiveness. I was deeply moved, and realized that I could not hold on to my hatred any longer.

Child abuse is perhaps the most difficult thing in the world to forgive. The victim – the child – is always completely innocent, whereas the perpetrator – the adult – is always completely guilty. Why should the innocent forgive the guilty? Many victims of child abuse mistakenly believe that they share some of the blame: that they somehow brought on or even deserved the abuse. In fact, much of the power an abuser holds over his victim, even after the physical abuse itself has stopped, comes from this tragically misguided notion of complicity. It is part of the victimization. Wouldn't forgiving their abuser then imply that the victim was at least partly to blame?

Nothing, of course, could be further from the truth. Forgiveness is necessary simply because both victim and victimizer – who in most cases know one another, or are even related – are prisoners of a shared darkness. Both will remain bound in this darkness until someone opens the door. Forgiveness is the only way out, and if our abuser chooses to remain in the darkness, that should not hold us back. If we leave the door open, he or she may even follow us out into the light.

KATE, A BRUDERHOF GRANDMOTHER, was also abused as a child. After facing her own feelings, however, she found she could become reconciled with her mother, who then had a change of heart:

> I was born in a small Canadian town shortly after World War II, the oldest child of a family of Russian Mennonite background. We were small farmers in a homesteading village, and conditions were extremely primitive.
>
> After my father sold our farm, he had to go into the city every day to work. Father's construction job was twenty-five miles away, and after his twelve-hour work-day he still had to work the small piece of land that was left to us.

We were four children, all girls. There were underly-
ing tensions in our family, but we couldn't explain them.
When my brother was born, nine years after me, things
became worse. Mother stayed home less and less. We
didn't realize it then, but she had started drinking.

Soon Kate's mother began to come home drunk, and after
that her parents separated. There was no family life to speak
of; the house was neglected, and the laundry was never
washed. Everything depended on thirteen-year-old Kate.

When Jamie, the youngest, started school, Mother was
almost never at home. I never managed to do any home-
work and was not learning very much. I completely
failed ninth grade and had to repeat it the following year.

My two younger sisters left home, found jobs, and
shared an apartment in town. But I stayed. Somebody
had to look after the little ones. And as poorly as I did it,
at least they were given something to eat.

In our town, hospitals for mentally and physically
handicapped adults were crowded, and the government
began to farm out people who didn't need full-time care
to local families. This seemed a good source of income
for our family, and Mother took in two older men and
a woman.

I had to give up my bed to one of the men and share a
double bed with the woman, who very often didn't sleep,
but when I told Mother that I couldn't cope with this
and wanted the hospital to take her back, she disagreed.
After all, there was a check coming in every month. She
said she would come home in the evenings to help me.
But the state she came home in! Then she'd say that if it

wasn't for me, she wouldn't be in such a mess.

At first I couldn't understand what she meant, but later I learned that my parents had been forced to marry because mother was already carrying me. At times she became physically abusive. In the morning, if she asked me about the bruises on my face and I told her she had done it, she claimed I was lying.

At sixteen, Kate quit school in order to devote herself totally to the care of her siblings. Around that time, she met Tom, her future husband; they married two years later. She still remembers the guilt she felt when her mother asked accusingly, "Who is going to do the work around here?" Nonetheless, Kate moved out of the house, and soon she and Tom were raising a family of their own.

At this point I just wanted to forget about my mother. I had my own little family, and I had Tom's parents, who loved my children. Suddenly my mother wanted contact, but I found plenty of reasons for not visiting her. I finally had some leverage, and I was going to pay her back.

By this time my parents' divorce was finalized. Mother eventually stopped drinking; she had come to realize that the combination of alcohol and blood-pressure medications would kill her. All the same, I was reluctant to have contact with her. I simply could not trust her.

A few years later, the couple joined the Bruderhof. Kate was expecting another child, and Tom invited her mother to share in the baby's arrival.

I was hopping mad and would have nothing to do with it. I told Tom, "You call her right back and tell her not to come; tell her whatever you want to tell her. This is my baby, and I'm not willing to share it with her." I was quite nasty about it. In the end, I went to one of the leaders of our community, and we sat down and talked about it.

He listened to me quietly and then said, "You have to come to peace with your mother."

I said, "You don't know my mother."

He replied, "That has nothing to do with it."

In the end, my mother did come. She was not well when she arrived and needed a lot of care. I didn't make it easy for her, but finally we were able to talk. Then, during the last few days before she went home, I sensed that there was something she was trying to tell me. More than that, she even seemed willing to listen to what I had to say to her. She wanted a new relationship – by then I desperately wanted it, too – and she was determined to remove whatever was in the way. At that point I realized she was not even aware of what she had done. When I was able to forgive her, both of us were healed.

In the loving atmosphere of her home, Kate made peace with her mother. She was able to forgive tremendous hurts from the past, but she also made an important recognition: it wasn't only her mother's lack of love, but also her own understandable coldness that had kept them apart for so many years.

NOT ALL CASES of parent-child estrangement are so black and white. Susan, a woman from California, comes from very different circumstances, and never suffered real abuse at the hands of her parents. Like Kate, however, she was bitter toward her mother for many years and began to find healing in their relationship only when she was able to forgive.

Ever since I can remember, I have had a difficult relationship with my mother. I feared her angry outbursts, her biting, sarcastic tongue, and never felt able to please her. As a consequence I felt angry toward her – a deep, smoldering, hidden anger that made me close myself off to her. I nursed hurts of remembered injustices from early childhood, of sharp words and a few blows (none worth remembering). I became extremely sensitive to her reproof and easily felt rejected.

Somehow we just never had an open, sharing relationship. Instead I looked to the other adults in my life, especially my teachers. My mother resented my attachment to my teachers but was never able to express it. I can remember wishing to be taken out of my family, to be adopted by one of them. I can also remember a strong physical feeling of not belonging that would come over me in waves.

In my desire to be accepted, I tried to be "good" and hid my true feelings. It probably didn't help that we were never allowed to answer back or say no to our parents or any adult. As children, we were to be seen and not heard.

It only became worse as I grew into adolescence. I found more and more ways subtly to act out my anger and do what I wanted to do. I also found more ways to sneak around my mother and, in a sense, "get back." It contributed in a large part to my having a secret, adulterous relationship with our parish priest, who often socialized with my parents.

That relationship eventually ended, and I married another man, but I continued to be at odds with my mother. It was actually a very strange relationship, because I still desperately wanted to please her.

Mom went through extended times of physical and emotional crisis over those years, but I found it difficult to sympathize or even show much interest. I finally reached out to her when she was going through a twelve-step program for alcoholism. We had a wonderful week of sharing, but the doors closed soon thereafter. I blamed it on her, though I cannot now say why.

Finally it became clear to me that her strong, self-confident, in-control exterior was just a shell for a very insecure person who was nursing a lot of hurt from her own childhood. We were both trying to reach out to one another in our own way, but both of us were afraid of rejection and so our efforts were superficial at best. I'm ashamed to say that I just stopped talking after two weeks.

The breakthrough came a few years later when I was hounded by a friend to listen to some tapes of talks by someone called Charles Stanley. Although I had never heard of him, I was looking for answers to many of my questions in life, so I listened guardedly. I can't remember exactly what he said, but it was just what I needed to hear at the time. I came to see my own share of guilt in the relationship, and the need for me to ask for forgiveness and to give it.

Not long after that I visited my parents. When I was alone with my mother, I asked her to forgive my actions in the past and told her I forgave her too. I admitted that I had been angry at her all of my life, even though I wasn't sure why. She didn't understand why I should be angry, but she too apologized for the hurt she had caused. She said, "What has happened has happened, and I can't change that; but we have to move on now." It was a time of healing for both of us. It allowed me to open up, be honest, and express my heart's desire to love and to be loved for who I was, not for what I thought I could give.

As soon as they faced their anger, Susan and her mother were able to start rebuilding their relationship. Many others with similar stories continue to suffer needlessly, because they cannot forgive. Who we are or where we are from isn't important. What matters is that we learn to forgive. Then miracles can happen. Painful memories will still arise on occasion to muddy the water, but we cannot allow them to cloud our vision forever. Even where forgetting is – and should be – impossible, we must believe that forgiveness is not only possible, but necessary. In forgiving we find true healing.

10 Forgiving Ourselves

WITHOUT BEING FORGIVEN, released from the consequences of what we have done, our capacity to act would, as it were, be confined to a single deed from which we could never recover; we would remain the victims of its consequences forever, not unlike the sorcerer's apprentice who lacked the magic formula to break the spell.

Hannah Arendt

EVEN IF WE ARE FORGIVEN by others, can we ever forgive ourselves? Many people are so tormented by their own actions that they no longer believe in the possibility of healing, but even these troubled souls can find hope.

Delf Fransham, a Canadian Quaker, found freedom from his past by showing love to others. Like many whose stories are told in this book, he was hit unexpectedly by a tragedy that changed his life. Yet in a way, his story is very different: the person he had to forgive was himself.

I first met Delf when I was thirteen. He moved to our South American community and began to teach in our school. There were eleven boys in my class, all of us ruffians, and only days after his arrival we decided to put him to the test.

It was a typical Paraguayan day – humid and around 100 degrees – and we offered to take him on a hike to see what he was made of. After leading him at least ten kilometers through jungle, prairie, and swampland, we finally turned back. Shortly after we arrived home he collapsed with heat stroke.

Delf was in bed for days, but we didn't care. We had achieved exactly what we wanted: we had proved him a "sissy." But we were in for a surprise. The day he came back to school, he said, "Boys, let's try that hike again." We couldn't believe it! We covered the same route again and, sure enough, this time he did not become sick. Delf won our respect and our hearts, and we trusted him from then on. We soon discovered that, far from being a sissy, he was a talented athlete. We loved to play soccer with him.

Decades later, and only by chance, I found out why Delf had poured so much love and energy into his work in our school. He had lost a son of his own in the most tragic of circumstances. Nicholas was born in April 1951, when the Franshams were living in Georgia. Shortly after Christmas 1952, he was playing outdoors when he ran towards a truck his father was backing into the driveway. The truck was loaded with firewood. Delf did not see his son until it was too late.

His wife, Katie, was talking to a neighbor inside the house when Delf carried their little boy in, limp in his arms. She remembers:

> I was beside myself – absolutely frantic – but Delf steadied me. We took our child to our doctor in Clarkesville, who was also the coroner, and explained what had happened...There was never any question about forgiving my husband, as I knew I was just as much to blame. Likewise he did not blame me, only himself. We stood in this sorrow together.

But Delf couldn't forgive himself, and the accident haunted him for years. From then on, he went out of his way to make time for children – time he could not spend with the son he had killed. Looking back, I remember how his eyes often glistened with tears, and I think now that he must have seen his son in us, or what his son might have been. His determination to pour himself out for others was his way of making up for the tragedy he had unwittingly caused. I am convinced that it saved him from brooding over his feelings of guilt. It gave him back his life, and finally a sense of peace.

Delf and Katie Fransham with Nicholas and Anna, 1952

DAVID HARVEY, now nearly seventy, joined the army at sixteen, just before the end of World War II. After spending most of the rest of the war years in training, he was transferred to Africa, then Germany, Italy, Hong Kong, China and the Mediterranean. At first he enjoyed his time in the army, especially the camaraderie he felt among fellow soldiers. But then something happened that changed his life forever.

> Part of my service time was spent in Kenya, predominantly carrying out police duties and hunting "terrorists." Much of the time was spent patrolling jungle areas. During one of these patrols I was involved in a terrible accident.
>
> While lying in wait for a band of "terrorists," we ourselves were ambushed. There was a lot of shooting and a lot of confusion, and misunderstood orders. The patrol split into two halves. My half walked in a straight line along an animal path, while the second half cleared the bush on each side. Those in the bush overtook those on the path, and we consequently ended up firing at each other. Directly to my front, the bushes parted and I fired, shooting the patrol commander in the head. Abandoning our mission, we carried the wounded man for sixteen hours through the jungle on a makeshift bamboo stretcher to get him the medical help he so desperately required.
>
> Eventually there was a court of inquiry and, in military terms, I was exonerated of all blame. But my conscience gave me no peace. Four years later, my term of service in the army ended and I returned to civilian life.

At first I found this very difficult. In the army I had been given a number instead of a name, trained to comply with any order without question, and to believe that anything I was told to do was correct. This did not fit in with civilian life. But slowly things returned to normal, and I had time to reminisce over my service career. The thing that always came to the forefront was the shooting of my comrade. Where was he? How was he? Had he even survived?

After a number of years, I started to make my own inquiries as to the whereabouts and welfare of my colleague. But all the avenues I tried drew a blank. I met ex-colleagues, each of whom had a different story as to what had become of him. Then in 1996 my wife, Marion, found a book which mentioned this very incident. I telephoned the author, who admitted that he hadn't seen him recently, but had heard that he was living in London.

I realized that I had drawn another blank. Frustrated, I decided to enlist the services of a local newspaper. They published my story and photograph in a weekly edition of their paper. Within forty-eight hours I had received a call from the person I had been seeking for years.

It was a difficult experience. After a number of telephone conversations, we arranged to meet each other at my house. In due course, he came bringing presents… to the man who had shot him! Because of me, he was paralyzed down one side and had difficulty walking and moving his arm. I asked him, "Can you ever forgive me?" He just hugged me. He had already forgiven me.

JOHN PLUMMER lives the quiet life of a Methodist pastor in a sleepy Virginia town these days, but things weren't always so. A helicopter pilot during the Vietnam War, he helped organize a napalm raid on the village of Trang Bang in 1972 – a bombing immortalized by the prize-winning photograph of one of its victims, Phan Thi Kim Phuc, shown on the cover of this book.

For the next twenty-four years, John was haunted by this picture, an image that for many people captured the essence of the war: a naked nine-year-old girl, burned, crying, arms outstretched, running toward the camera, with plumes of black smoke billowing in the sky behind her.

For twenty-four years his conscience tormented him. He badly wanted to find the girl, to say that he was sorry – but he could not. At least as a country, Vietnam was a closed chapter for him; he could never bring himself to go there again. Friends tried to reassure him. Hadn't he done everything within his power to see that the village was cleared of civilians? But still he found no peace. He turned in on himself, his marriage failed, and he began to drink.

Then, in an almost unbelievable coincidence, on Veterans Day 1996, John met Kim at the Vietnam Memorial. Kim had come to Washington, D.C. to lay a wreath for peace; John had come with a group of former pilots still searching for freedom from the past. In a speech to the crowd, Kim said that she was not bitter. Although she still suffered immensely from her burns, she wanted people to know that others had suffered even more: "Behind that picture of me, thousands and thousands of people…died.

Phan Thi Kim Phuc and John Plummer, 1996

They lost parts of their bodies. Their whole lives were destroyed, and nobody took their picture."[16]

Kim went on to say that she forgave the men who had bombed her village, and that although she could not change the past, she now wanted to "promote peace." John, beside himself, pushed through the crowds and managed to catch her attention before she was whisked away by a police escort. He identified himself as the pilot responsible for bombing her village twenty years before, and they were able to talk for two short minutes.

> Kim saw my grief, my pain, my sorrow...She held out her arms to me and embraced me. All I could say was "I'm sorry; I'm sorry" – over and over again. And at the same time she was saying, "It's all right, I forgive you."[17]

They met again later the same day, and Kim reaffirmed her forgiveness. They have since become good friends, and call each other regularly.

Has John found the peace he was searching for? He says he has. Although his emotions are still easily stirred by memories of the war, he feels that he has now been able to forgive himself and put the event behind him.

John says that it was vital for him to meet face to face with Kim, to tell her that he had truly agonized over her injuries. All the same, he maintains that the forgiveness he has received is a gift – not something earned or even deserved. It is, finally, a mystery: he still can't quite grasp how a two-minute talk could wipe away a twenty-four-year nightmare.

RICHARD, ANOTHER Vietnam veteran, is a gentle, quiet man who loves children and horses. In the five years that I have known him, however, I have learned that he is tormented by events that happened more than two decades ago:

> Death is on my mind a lot. The deaths I have caused – and wanting my own death – are with me every day. I joke around a lot with the people I work with. I have to, to hide the pain, and to keep my mind from thinking. I need to laugh. Laughing keeps the blues away.
>
> But I cannot love. Part of my soul is missing, and it seems I won't ever get it back. I don't know if I can ever forgive myself for all of my wrongs. I live day to day, but I am tired all the time – tired. Will it ever end? I don't see how. It's been with me over twenty-five years now.

People like Richard are often rightly urged to receive formal counseling. They are advised to find others who have had similar experiences, to join support groups, or to attend group therapy. Richard has done all of this; he has seen more than his share of counselors and gone to group meetings with other Vietnam veterans for over a year. But still he has not found peace.

Therapy is often helpful, but sometimes it stops short of offering a lasting solution. A good psychotherapist can encourage you to reveal the burdens of your past, but unless it is followed by remorse and the recognition of a personal need for forgiveness, confession is useless.

Harvard psychiatrist Robert Coles recalls an important conversation he once had with Anna Freud. Although over-shadowed by her more famous father, Anna was a renowned psychoanalyst in her own right. Talking about an elderly woman's long and troubled psychological history, she sud-denly concluded:

> You know, before we say good-bye to this lady, we should wonder among ourselves not only what to think – we do that all the time! – but what in the world we would want for her. Oh, I don't mean psychotherapy! She's had lots of that. It would take more years, I suspect, of psycho-analysis than the good Lord has given her...No, she's had her fill of "us," even if she doesn't know it...This poor old lady doesn't need us at all...What she needs... is forgiveness. She needs to make peace with her soul, not talk about her mind. There must be a God, some-where, to help her, to hear her, to heal her...and we cer-tainly aren't the ones who will be of assistance to her in that regard![18]

This point is a vital one: we cannot find peace and healing unless we can learn to confront what we have done wrong.

Yet an admission of guilt is not enough by itself to achieve forgiveness. Sometimes the person we have wronged is unable or unwilling to forgive us. Sometimes we are unable or unwilling to forgive ourselves. Perhaps then, as Anna Freud suggests, we need to look to God for help. We receive forgiveness as a gift of love, reaching us at the very place where we feel least worthy to receive it. Only this gift can free us wholeheartedly to forgive others and commit ourselves to change.

11 Accepting Responsibility

IN THE CONFESSION of concrete sins the old man dies a painful, shameful death before the eyes of a brother. Because this humiliation is so hard, we continually scheme to avoid it. Yet in the deep mental and physical pain of humiliation before a brother we experience…our rescue and salvation.

Dietrich Bonhoeffer

IT IS IMPOSSIBLE to forgive unless we recognize our own need for forgiveness. Actually, mere recognition is not enough: we must acknowledge our faults to someone else.

Some people dismiss "confession" as a strange, meaningless Catholic ritual. Others admit that confession – whether to a priest, friend or counselor – can be useful, but that one can find peace of heart just as easily without it. Yet the peace of such people is often, as Tolstoy put it, nothing more than a "deadness of the soul."

Guilt works in secret, and it loses its power only when it is allowed out into the open. Often our desire to come across as strong and virtuous keeps us from admitting to others the things we've done wrong. Instead, we try to blot out our wrongdoing from memory, and when that doesn't work we simply try to keep it hidden. Yet by doing this we only pile guilt upon guilt. Unless we own up to what we've done wrong and accept responsibility, the pressure can become overwhelming.

Being sorry for what we've done wrong has nothing to do with self-torment. If we look only at ourselves, we are sure to despair. Once we have cried our tears of remorse, we must stand back and allow the muddy waters of our hearts to clear – otherwise we will never see to the bottom of anything.

STEVE, AN OLD FRIEND who grew up in suburban Washington, D.C. in the 1960s, writes:

> In my search for peace and wholeness, I pursued various religions and studied psychology, but I received only partial answers…Not until I finally saw how wrong my own life was did I recognize how urgently I needed to change.
>
> The pivotal experience came unexpectedly, one day in 1983, when I first became fully aware of the enormous avalanche of wrongs I had committed. Before

that, this reality had been hidden by pride and by wanting to look good in front of others. But now images and memories poured out of me like a river of bile.

All I wanted was to be free, to have nothing dark and ugly hidden in the depths of me; I wanted to make good, wherever I could, the wrongs I had done. I had no excuses for myself – youth, circumstances, or bad peers. I was responsible for what I had done.

On one page after another I poured it all out in clear detail. I felt as though an angel of repentance was slashing at my heart with his sword, such was the pain. I wrote dozens of letters to people and organizations I had cheated, stolen from, and lied to…Finally I felt truly free.

In *The Brothers Karamazov*, the great Russian novelist Dostoevsky wrote in the same vein about a man who confesses to a murder he has kept hidden for decades: "I feel joy and peace for the first time after so many years. There is heaven in my heart…Now I dare to love my children and to kiss them."[19]

TRUE FORGIVENESS SPREADS from one person to the next, and has the power to sweep through an entire community, town or region.

The people of Möttlingen, a village in Germany's Black Forest, experienced such a movement in 1844, and it turned their lives upside down. Möttlingen is an ordinary place today, and it was no different then. In fact, its now-famous pastor, Johann Christoph Blumhardt, often sighed about the apathy that had been lying like a blanket of fog over his parish. But a plaque on the half-timbered wall of an old house attests to the remarkable events that once swept the village off its feet: "O man, think on eternity, and mock not the time of grace; for judgment is at hand!"

The "awakening," as it is often referred to today, began on New Year's Eve 1843, when a young man known for his wild carousing and violent temper came to the rectory door. After pleading to see the pastor, he was let in. He told Blumhardt that he hadn't slept for a whole week, and feared he would die if he couldn't unburden his conscience. Blumhardt remained somewhat cautious, only accepting the man's sincerity when he began pouring out a torrent of misdeeds, large and small.

Thus began a remarkable wave of remorse. By January 27, 1844, sixteen people had come to the rectory to unburden their hearts. Three days later, the number had risen to thirty-five. Ten days later, it was up to more than one hundred and fifty. Men and women from all the surrounding villages poured into Möttlingen.

There was nothing of the emotionalism of religious "revivals," no exaggerated proclamations of past wickedness or public avowals of repentance. The awakening was too sober and earnest for that, too deeply rooted in reality. People felt an inner compulsion to break with their past: their hearts were pierced, and they suddenly saw themselves in all of their ugliness. Horrified, they felt they simply had to put their old ways behind them.

Most significant, this movement of hearts went beyond words and emotions and produced concrete expressions of repentance and forgiveness. Stolen goods were returned, enemies reconciled, infidelities and crimes (including a case of infanticide) confessed, and broken marriages restored. Even the town drunks stayed away from the taverns!

Those who question the authenticity of the Möttlingen awakening need only look at its results to see that it was no fabrication. Although ridiculed by people from other towns, almost the whole village was affected. In 1883, almost forty years later, Blumhardt's biographer, Friedrich Zündel, wrote that it had not yet been forgotten – even the children of those involved still radiated joy. Over the last thirty years I have traveled to Germany several times to visit Blumhardt's granddaughters. (My parents, both strongly influenced by his writings, named me after him.) I can testify that something of the same spirit that once swept the town off its feet remains even today.

Was the awakening in Möttlingen an isolated event? Could it happen again? Blumhardt had faith that it could: after all, it started with just one remorseful man.

IN MANY INSTANCES a wrong can be put right by a simple apology – for example, when we have been short with someone or otherwise lacked compassion. In my experience, however, willful acts such as deceit or theft must not only be confessed, but their consequences faced, if there is to be full freedom. There are instances where more than private confession is necessary.

As Stanley Hauerwas writes, "A community cannot afford to 'overlook' one another's sins because they have learned that sins are a threat to being a community of peace." Members of a united community will no longer harbor their grievances as theirs alone. "When we think our brother or sister has sinned against us, such an affront is not just against us but against the whole community."[20]

Mark and Debbie, friends of mine now living in Pennsylvania, experienced this firsthand in a small California community they belonged to in the late 1980s:

> Over the years we witnessed the disastrous results of ignoring wrongdoing or secretly hiding it. We lived in a small urban community with several people, one of whom was a single man who had fallen in love with a married woman in our group. Some of us tried to tackle their affair by talking with them separately about it. Yet there was no way to really "bring it out in the open."
>
> Afraid of being judgmental, we chose to believe that this wasn't a very serious matter, at least not serious enough to bring it out into the open. Didn't we all make mistakes? Who were we to judge? We convinced ourselves that confrontation would not only add to their sense of shame and self-condemnation, but also perpetuate the cycle of failure. So we avoided it like the plague. Now we see that it was this so-called "compassion" that did the perpetuating.
>
> The man eventually left anyway. Two years later, the woman also left the community – and divorced her husband.

Mark and Debbie's experience is surely not unique. A marriage was allowed to fail because everyone tried to ignore what was really going on. Confrontation is sometimes essential if there is to be forgiveness, since until someone comes face to face with what they've been doing wrong, they can neither seek nor experience forgiveness. Refusal to confront people who are hurting others – because we convince ourselves that it's none of our business, for example – can sometimes be little more than a way of excusing people for the things they do wrong. And as we've already seen, excusing wrongdoing and forgiving it are opposites.

IN HIS NOVEL *Too Late the Phalarope*, Alan Paton writes of a respected Afrikaner who, at the height of apartheid, commits an "unpardonable" sin: fornication with a black woman. When this is brought to light, his family is devastated. His friends leave him, his relatives spurn him, and his father dies in shame. Yet a neighbor agonizes over what his response should be:

> An offender can be punished…But to punish and not to restore, that is the greatest of all offenses…If a man takes unto himself God's right to punish, then he must also take upon himself God's promise to restore.[21]

Confession paves the way for forgiveness and reconciliation. Without it, we remain deadlocked in our pride, and forgiving is simply not possible. When my father-in-law Hans came back to the Bruderhof after eleven years away, he wrote:

> I expected that bricks would be thrown, but nothing like that happened. I was given every opportunity to bring up my questions and misgivings openly, and

everyone spoke quite openly to me. But what melted my heart was not just the openness; rather, it was a love that shared responsibility – a love that was prepared to forgive because it had itself experienced forgiveness.

It was not a question of a fight between people, but a fight against the thing that separated us. In short, everyone sat on the same bench. Things were not smeared over in a sentimental way, but even the most painful facts were recognized in the light of love.

Hans was touched by the love of his community, but what broke his stubbornness was their willingness to ask his forgiveness for where they had failed him.

Sarah, another member of our community, writes of the joy and freedom she experienced when she decided to clean her slate and make a fresh start:

> I could hardly sleep at night. Something was hammering in my head: I had to put things right! I went to some trusted friends and told them everything. It helped so much to do that, even though what I had to confess was sickening. In the days that followed, things kept coming to mind, and again I couldn't wait. I remember running to tell them. When you clean your slate, even the smallest thing is no longer insignificant. I had to get rid straight away of every little thing that came to mind. I could not wait.
>
> I never knew I would find such a joy in confession and repentance. My heart got lighter and lighter.

Like many others who have found the strength to face up to their misdeeds and ask for forgiveness, Sarah discovered a wonderful sense of release. She had expected other community members to disapprove strongly of what she had done in the past, and to avoid her completely once she told them about it. But to her surprise she found that they welcomed her honesty and accepted her with all her failings. In admitting responsibility for past wrongs, and in stating a determination to make a new start, Sarah found – as each of us can – that confession paved the way for reconciliation.

12 Forgiving God

IT IS NOT RIGHT to try to remove all suffering, nor is it right to endure it stoically. Suffering can be used, turned to good account. What makes a life happy or unhappy is not outward circumstances, but our inner attitude to them.

Eberhard Arnold

WHEN WE SPEAK OF FORGIVENESS, we usually speak of forgiving the hurts we do to each other, but there are times when there just doesn't seem to be anyone to blame. Since the emotions we experience at times like this are often the same as those we experience when there clearly is a guilty party, many of us – rightly or wrongly – tend to blame God for allowing us to suffer without apparent reason or justification. Full of anger and pain, we ask: "How can a merciful God permit this?" Can we "forgive" God?

I don't intend to look at whether or not it is fair to blame God in circumstances like these. In many ways, it is easier to blame God and forgive him – even if we don't actually believe in him – than to face the possibility that there really might be no one to blame. Anger is a legitimate stage of grief, even when there's no obvious target for us to direct this anger at. We need to express our anger and deal with it if we are to stand any chance of finding proper healing and moving on.

So can we learn to forgive God when we hold him responsible for hurting us, just as we learn to forgive other people when we feel hurt by them? The solution lies in our developing a willingness to learn from our experiences, to grow from them and produce something positive out of what can otherwise seem like an entirely negative time of our lives. Where there appears to be no reason for our suffering, we need to give it one. A crisis need not only be a disaster: it can also be an opportunity.

ZOHAR CHAMBERLAIN, a friend from Kibbutz Kishor in Israel, lost her leg in an accident when she was only seventeen. Although Zohar had no one to blame for what happened, and therefore no one to forgive, she was still angry about her circumstances and deeply frustrated at suddenly having to learn to do things she had always done without even a second thought.

It was the summer of 1987. I was seventeen years old and going to do a year of service as a guide with a youth organization in Jerusalem. Only four days after I began, I had to travel north, and so I took a bus from Jerusalem's central bus station. It was the most sensible thing to do. I didn't hitchhike or take any other risks. I just went as a passenger.

It didn't take more than a few minutes to drive down to Yirmiyahu Street, and there wasn't even a chance for the driver to really speed, but the road was slippery with water and soap from one of the restaurants on the side. It appears that the driver made a mistake and locked up the brakes. The bus went sliding into a parked truck. Eighteen people were injured, and a soldier and a five-year-old girl were killed.

I do not remember anything from the accident, though the paramedic who started treating me straight away said that I had remained conscious. I only vaguely remember a few details from the hospital: giving my ID number and the phone numbers needed to notify my parents; my clothes being cut off; my mother on the way from the recovery room to the Intensive Care Unit.

It wasn't until the day after that I was told I had lost a leg. My mother came to my bed and asked if I knew what had happened. I said that something was wrong with my legs, but I couldn't see them as I was lying flat on my back. I don't think I was in shock, but that was probably due to all the painkillers. I stayed in ICU for twelve days. I felt quite protected, even though I suffered from terrible pains, could hardly lift my head off the pillow and had a high fever almost all of the time. I was being looked after, wasn't expected to deal with anything as yet, and had all the support and loving care I could possibly wish for.

Then, just before the Jewish New Year, I was moved to the orthopedic ward. They decided that my right knee could not be saved, and told me I had to undergo a second operation to amputate my leg just above it. This was much harder to take, and I broke into tears when I told a good friend who had come to see me.

The process of recovering from this second operation was difficult. I suffered especially from phantom pains in the missing leg. What made it more difficult was the doctors trying to tell me that such things don't exist. That period of about four weeks was a time of great helplessness for me. I was aware of my weakness and inability to look after myself (my family and friends were by my side all the time), and it actually made me very angry. I had been a very independent person, and all of a sudden I was a baby again. It wasn't easy having to pull up the strength to do things that used to be taken for granted and now seemed nearly impossible.

I don't know what sort of a person I would have become if it weren't for this accident and the experiences that followed it, but I believe it made me stronger. In a way, realizing that I needed others around me and having to deal with this has made the importance of community very clear to me. Rather than feeling useless because I can't do certain things, I've found that admitting I need help has made me more of a whole person. Where before I had tended to look down on those who couldn't live up to life's demands on their own, I've had a good lesson in accepting other people as they are through learning to ask for help.

IN MY OWN LIFE, I've often had to face frustrating situations and have sometimes felt like blaming God. On one occasion, I had been on a fishing trip in upstate New York – unsuccessful as far as the catch was concerned, but a welcome opportunity to escape the pressures of work for a few days.

On the way home I noticed that I was losing my voice. I ignored it at first, expecting it to improve within several days. It did not, so I was soon referred to a specialist, who diagnosed a paralyzed vocal chord. He reassured me that my voice would eventually recover, but weeks and then months went by, and there was no change. His prescription was complete voice rest – I wasn't even allowed to whisper. I wondered if I would ever speak again.

To make things worse, our community was in desperate need of strong leadership at the time. We were in the middle of a crisis of sorts – a period of intense soul-searching – and throughout the weeks of lively and sometimes contentious discussion, I could only sit by in silence.

I yearned to be able to participate in these meetings, but could not; for the first time, I realized what a gift speech really is. Frustrated and discouraged, I couldn't even talk to my wife and children, but had to write everything down for them. To be honest, I was angry. As a Christian leader, I could not understand why God should seemingly have silenced me at a time when I was so clearly needed.

Three months later, my voice began to return; now, five years later, it is nearly normal. But I have never forgotten those twelve weeks. Looking back, I can see that my inability to speak helped me to develop a more humble and flexible outlook on life. I have gradually learned to take stock of my own shortcomings and to make the best of an imperfect situation. I am reminded of that time whenever I'm tempted to blame God in moments of crisis or frustration.

ANDREA, A WOMAN in our community, struggled to accept quite different circumstances: she suffered through three miscarriages before having a healthy child. At times, she found her burdens were too heavy to bear.

> Neil and I were delighted to find that I was pregnant after only six months of marriage. But one night, just before Christmas, I felt intense pain that grew rapidly worse. Our doctor wanted to send me to the hospital, and our neighbor, a nurse, came to stay with me until we left for town. She confirmed my worst fears – I would probably lose my baby. The emotional pain was at least as severe as the physical. Why, God? Why me? Why do you have to take away this tiny soul so soon? What have I done wrong?
>
> In order to save my life, an operation was necessary. The baby was lost, and I spent weeks recuperating. What a different Christmas this had become!
>
> We agonized over our loss and felt alone in our pain. When one of our relatives said to us, "Cheer up! Maybe you'll have better luck next time," I felt like I had been slapped in the face. Luck? We had just lost a baby, a real person, our child!

Someone sent me a card that said, "The Lord giveth, and the Lord taketh away, blessed be the name of the Lord." That made me really upset. How could I thank God for this horrible, painful experience? I couldn't. And I couldn't stop thinking that somehow God was punishing me, even though I couldn't understand why.

Our pastor consoled me: God is a God of love, not of punishment, and he is there to ease our pain. I grasped onto his words as a drowning person grabs onto a pole held out from the shore. Neil's loving support seemed like a visible sign of this love, and we discovered that our pain united us in a new way. The words, "Weeping shall endure for the night, but joy cometh in the morning," especially comforted me, even when I couldn't feel that joy coming, when it seemed that dawn would never break.

Slowly, with time and with the loving help of those around me, I was able to feel that this deeply painful experience had given me an inkling of the love of God, who cares about the suffering of people and who was, I am convinced, right there beside me in my pain. God became more real to me, and I began to trust his love.

But then, some months later, when I was expecting another baby and hoping fervently that all would go well, the same thing happened again. Severe pain, an emergency trip to the hospital, and an operation to save my life. Again another precious little person lost just after it had come into being. Deep pain tore my heart apart. I wrote in my diary: "I cannot see why; perhaps I never will. I need the assurance of faith – Help me!"

Neil stood faithfully beside me. He had lost a sister to cancer some years before, and what he had written then was a great source of sustenance: "We are separated from God only in physical distance, and that distance is perhaps not great." I hung on to that with all my strength.

Slowly, over weeks and months, the pain of loss lessened, although it has never departed entirely. About a year later we again lost a little unborn baby. Once more there was deep pain in my heart, but this time no desperation over why.

Today Andrea is the mother of a beautiful eight-year-old daughter. Although the memory of her first three pregnancies brings back a flood of emotions, she is not bitter. She tries to see something positive in her suffering, and feels that because of it, she not only loves her husband more deeply, having gone through hell and back with him, but she also treasures her daughter more than she might have done otherwise.

JONATHAN AND GRETCHEN RHOADS, a young couple in our community, were married in 1995. Like any new parents they eagerly awaited the birth of their first child. Alan was born after a seemingly normal pregnancy, and it was only after he was discharged from the hospital that his parents noticed something was wrong. He didn't eat well and his muscle tone was poor. He lay very still, almost without moving, and when he breathed, he occasionally made strange gurgling sounds. He was quickly admitted to a nearby university hospital, but he was three months old before his problems became clear: he would probably never walk or talk; he was blind; and he had significant abnormalities of the hips, brain, ears and stomach.

Alan's parents were devastated. They had long suspected that something was wrong, but they hadn't expected it to be this bad. Right away they began to accuse themselves, and it wasn't long before they began to accuse God: why us?

Jonathan once told me that he was angry, but on closer questioning he couldn't say at whom his anger was directed. At himself? Gretchen? The doctors? God? Yes, perhaps, though he couldn't explain why.

> One of the things you learn quickly is not to compare your child to others. Our neighbor's baby is as heavy as Alan, yet he is only a third of Alan's age. He has no trouble downing a bottle in fifteen minutes. For us, every half-ounce is a major victory. Why? There is nothing to say. Either God hates us, or this is just how Alan is meant to be. We may never know why, but if we are resentful, we will kill any joys we might have had.

When they turned to me in their need, I assured Jonathan and Gretchen that they were in no way responsible for their son's suffering. I told them that while every child is a gift from God, Alan is perhaps a very special one, for he can teach us valuable lessons about patience and compassion. Like all children born with some form of disability, he reminds us about what really matters in life, drawing us out of the rat race and helping us to get our priorities straight. Children like Alan have an ability to bring out the best in us, putting us back in touch with our real selves.

Gretchen and Alan Rhoads, 1997

Alan's parents still struggle to forgive. It isn't easy. There are times when they want to run away, when they simply can't face another visitor offering meaningless words of sympathy.

As Alan approaches his first birthday, they are once again faced with uncertainties. Recent developments have included a tracheostomy and feeding tubes, and on top of that, an appendectomy. How much more suffering will he have to endure?

In a world that offers "early diagnosis" (and subsequent termination) as the answer to imperfect babies, Alan's parents are witnesses to the intrinsic worth of every child. He is not, they point out, a genetic anomaly. He is a person who has a great deal to tell us, and they are not about to let him go. Gretchen writes:

> His small hand reaches up through a tangle of wires to find my cheek. As I stoop to lift him from his bed, his eyelids lift slightly and he gives me a sleepy grin...In the eleven months since his birth, Alan has been hospital-

ized five times; we have long since stopped counting the
outpatient appointments. Each time we come home with
more questions and fewer answers; more tears, and less
certainty. But as he snuggles against me and looks around
curiously, he grins. His acceptance is balm to my heart.

How much more pain can he bear? What new hurdles
await us? His tracheostomy has taken away the few small
adventures we had looked forward to: bottles, and the
chance to explore solid food. No more gurgles of joy,
either, and no more cries of frustration.

If he lives, the doctor tells us, he may outgrow the
need for these tubes. *If he lives.* The words cut to our
hearts, and yet his smile continues to give us hope. He
is teaching us acceptance – and thus forgiveness – every
day.

Epilogue
All Things New

THOUGH JUSTICE be thy plea, consider this:
That in the course of justice none of us
Should see salvation. We do pray for mercy,
And that same prayer doth teach us all to render
The deeds of mercy.

William Shakespeare

FORGIVENESS IS POWER. It frees us from our past, overcoming every evil. It can heal both the person forgiving and the person forgiven. In fact, it could change the world if we would only allow it to flow through us unchecked. But how often we stand in its way, not daring to unleash its force! We hold the keys to forgiveness in our hands, and we must choose whether or not to use them every day.

In the last year I have met twice with a man on Connecticut's death row. Michael Ross, thirty-seven, is a Cornell graduate. He is also a serial killer and rapist. No one can deny the horror of his crimes, nor can anyone presume to speak for the families of his victims. To do so would, at the very least, belittle or gloss over the immense suffering they continue to bear. But neither must we fail to see that Michael, too, longs desperately for forgiveness and healing:

> I feel a profound sense of guilt: an intense, overwhelming, and pervasive guilt that surrounds my soul with dark, tormenting clouds of self-hatred, remorse, and sorrow…Reconciliation is what I yearn for most: reconciliation with the spirit of my victims, with their families and friends, and finally with myself and God.

Can we turn our backs on such a man? Should we not rather confront him as a fellow human being with the horror of what he has done?

At the beginning of this book, I wrote about a man who had murdered a seven-year-old girl. I asked, can such a man be forgiven? In the months since I first met him, this man has undergone a remarkable change. Whereas at first he was emotionally numb and saw his crime as the inevitable, if awful, result of society's ills, he has now begun to accept responsibility for his own actions. And he has begun to agonize over his own need for change and forgiveness – to weep for others, rather than for himself. In meeting this man, I have seen him confront the evil of his crime and slowly begin to admit responsibility and show remorse.

Can such a man be forgiven? If we truly believe in the transforming power of forgiveness, we must believe that he can. We must never, of course, belittle or condone his crime. But we must also not deny him the opportunity to change. Ultimately, as Martin Luther King saw, forgiveness has the potential to turn an enemy into a friend. Indeed, forgiveness has transformed the lives of those whose stories are told in this book. It transformed the small town of Möttlingen in the 1840s. We must believe that it can transform the whole world today.

Notes

1   C. S. Lewis, *Readings for Meditation and Reflection,* ed. by Walter Hooper (New York: HarperCollins, 1996), 63.

2   Gordon Wilson with Alf McCreary, *Marie: A Story from Enniskillen.* (London: Marshall Pickering, 1991), 92–93.

3   Ibid.

4   Steven and Patti Ann McDonald with E. J. Kahn, *The Steven McDonald Story* (New York: Donald I Fine, 1989), 133–136.

5   *The Words of Martin Luther King, Jr,* Selected and Introduced by Coretta Scott King (New York: Newmarket Press, 1983), 23.

6   Martin Luther King, Jr, *Strength To Love* (London: Fount, 1977), 47–48, 51–52. Adapted to inclusive language.

7   Ibid, 48, 54–55. Adapted to inclusive language.

8   Robert Coles, "The Inexplicable Prayers of Ruby Bridges," quoted by Donald W. Shriver in *Studies: An Irish Quarterly Review* (vol. 78, no. 310, summer 1989), 148–149.

9   Naim Stifan Ateek, *Justice, and Only Justice: A Palestinian Theology of Liberation* (Maryknoll, NY: Orbis Books, 1989), 68–69.

10   Quoted by Carol J. Birkland in *Studies: An Irish Quarterly Review* (vol. 78, no. 310, summer 1989), 167.

11   C. S. Lewis, *Fern Seed and Elephants, and Other Essays on Christianity* (London: Fount, 1977), 40–42.

[12] M. Scott Peck, *The Different Drum: Community Making and Peace* (New York: Simon & Schuster, 1987), 226–227.

[13] C. S. Lewis, *Readings for Meditation and Reflection,* ed. by Walter Hooper (New York: HarperCollins, 1996), 130.

[14] Joan Winmill Brown, ed., *The Martyred Christian: 160 Readings from Dietrich Bonhoeffer* (New York: Collier/ Macmillan, 1983), 107.

[15] C. S. Lewis, *Readings for Meditation and Reflection,* ed. by Walter Hooper (New York: HarperCollins, 1996), 63–64.

[16] *Christian Century,* February 19, 1997, 182–184.

[17] Ibid.

[18] Robert Coles, *Harvard Diary: Reflections on the Sacred and the Secular* (New York: Crossroads, 1990), 177–180.

[19] Fyodor Dostoyevsky, *The Brothers Karamazov,* translated by Constance Garnett (New York: The Modern Library, n.d.), 373.

[20] Stanley M. Hauerwas, *Christian Existence Today: Essays on Church, World, and Living in Between* (Durham, NC: Labyrinth Press, 1988), 91.

[21] Alan Paton, *Too Late the Phalarope* (New York: Charles Scribner's Sons, 1953), 264–265.

The Bruderhof

THE BRUDERHOF is an international Christian movement committed to a life of simplicity, community and nonviolence. Like the early Christians, and like other well-established religious movements through history, Bruderhof members forsake private property in favor of more communal forms of ownership. They voluntarily pool not only their money and possessions, but their time and talents as well. At the heart of their commitment is a deep-seated dedication to service, love of neighbor and family, and faithfulness to the teachings of Jesus.

Founded in Germany in 1920 by the scholar Eberhard Arnold, the Bruderhof ("place of brothers") trace their heritage back to the Anabaptist and Hutterian movements of 16th-Century Europe. Forced to leave Nazi Germany in 1937, they found refuge in England before settling in Latin America. The first American community opened in 1954, and by the early 1960s all Bruderhof members had moved to the United States or England. There are currently five Bruderhof communities in the northeastern USA and two in southeastern England, with a total membership of around 2,500 men, women and children.

The Bruderhof is involved in a wide range of social service and community action activities, ranging from prison visiting to working with homeless people. They are active opponents of the death penalty and have long been energetic in promoting justice, peace, and reconciliation in both politics and personal life, especially in the areas of race relations and interreligious dialogue.

While many descendants of the original Bruderhof remain in the community, membership is open to any adult seeking a faith-based life of simplicity and service. All members work without pay, and with a commitment to brotherly-sisterly relationships with their co-workers. Guests are welcome, and Bruderhof communities host thousands of visitors every year, from all creeds and backgrounds.

For more information, visit the Bruderhof website: www.bruderhof.org or write to:

Spring Valley Bruderhof
Rte 381 North
Farmington PA 15437-9506

In the UK, write to:

Darvell Bruderhof
Robertsbridge
E. Sussex TN32 5DR

Other Titles from Plough

A Little Child Shall Lead Them
Johann Christoph Arnold

A welcome approach to child rearing based on the biblical idea of "becoming a child" and – building on that – bringing up children with reverence for their childlikeness. **$10.00/£7.00**

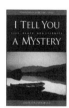

I Tell You A Mystery: Life, Death, and Eternity
Johann Christoph Arnold

Drawing on stories of real people, Arnold addresses the universal human fear of aging and purposelessness, and shows that even today, in our culture of isolation and death, there is such a thing as hope. **$12.00/£8.00**

The Gospel in Dostoyevsky
Edited by the Bruderhof

An introduction to the "great God-haunted Russian" comprised of passages from *The Brothers Karamazov*, *Crime and Punishment*, and *The Idiot.* **$15.00/£10.00**

Why We Live in Community
Eberhard Arnold

with two interpretive talks by Thomas Merton. Inspirational thoughts on the basis, meaning, and purpose of community. **$7.00/£5.00**

To order, or to request a complete catalog, call 800-521-8011.
In the UK, call 0800 269 048.
Visit our website at www.plough.com.

Prices subject to change without notice.